BLACK GLASSES LIKE CLARK KENT

Also by Terese Svoboda

Fiction

Tin God
Trailer Girl and Other Stories
A Drink Called Paradise
Cannibal

Poetry

Treason
Mere Mortals
Laughing Africa
All Aberration

Translation

Cleaned the Crocodile's Teeth

BLACK
GLASSES
LIKE
CLARK KENT

A GI'S SECRET FROM POSTWAR JAPAN

TERESE SVOBODA

Graywolf Press
SAINT PAUL, MINNESOTA

Publication of this volume is made possible in part by a grant provided by the Minnesota State Arts Board, through an appropriation
by the Minnesota State Legislature; a grant from the Wells Fargo
Foundation Minnesota; and a grant from the National Endowment
for the Arts, which believes that a great nation deserves great art.
Significant support has also been provided by the Bush Foundation;
Target; the McKnight Foundation; and other generous contributions
from foundations, corporations, and individuals. To these organizations and individuals we offer our heartfelt thanks.

MINNESOTA
STATE ARTS BOARD

NATIONAL
ENDOWMENT
FOR THE ARTS

TARGET.

The Graywolf Press Nonfiction Prize is funded in part by endowed
gifts from the Arsham Ohanessian Charitable Remainder Unitrust
and the Ruth Easton Fund of the Edelstein Family Foundation.

Published by Graywolf Press
2402 University Avenue, Suite 203
Saint Paul, Minnesota 55114
All rights reserved.

www.graywolfpress.org

Published in the United States of America

ISBN 978-1-55597-490-9

2 4 6 8 9 7 5 3 1
First Graywolf Printing, 2008

Library of Congress Control Number: 2007925191

Cover design: Kyle G. Hunter

Cover photos: From the collection of Frank Svoboda
Additional art: istockphoto.com

FOR DON

Guilt is always beyond doubt.

—FRANZ KAFKA

On TV and in the movies, Clark Kent always came across as a bit of a nuisance, nearly a joke, and smirky phrases like "mild-mannered" clung to him like iron filings around a funny face. But in an extreme instance of Coleridge's "willing suspension of disbelief for the moment," Kent's boxy black frames, along with his business suit, tie, and day job at the *Daily Planet*, completed the props of Superman's civilian disguise, though who, really, could have been fooled? In some later versions of the legend, Kent's glasses were themselves Kryptonite, fashioned from the spaceship that conveyed Superman to Earth so that the lenses might withstand the terrible force of his solar Heat Vision. Following the puzzling death of George Reeves (recently dramatized in the film *Hollywoodland*), and the melancholy fate of Christopher Reeve, any invocation of Superman inevitably summons a cliché "curse of Superman" as readily as "Superhero" or "Man of Steel."

Among novelists, filmmakers, and poets of the skittish, fledgling twenty-first century, classic comics tend to focus the cultural moves earlier generations once located in classical Greek and Roman mythology. "My uncle is Superman," Terese Svoboda declares at the outset of *Black Glasses Like Clark Kent*, her family romance in the guise of a revisionist American history—or is it American history as a revisionist family tragedy? "With black Clark Kent glasses, grapefruit-sized biceps, lots of brilliantined thick dark hair, and a solid jaw, six-four and as handsome as all get-out, he's the perfect match for Kryptonite."

Black Glasses Like Clark Kent probes a mystery (from the Greek root "to close the mouth or eyes") as Sigmund Freud and Dashiell Hammett, Patricia Highsmith and D. W. Winnicott, would have calculated the notion. If the ego, superego, and id of traditional psychological case studies supposedly mimic the three floors in a Viennese bourgeois abode, Svoboda's tale instead suggests a fever-dream horror house—her multistory structure is all angles, dead ends, ghosts, and trapdoors. As Private Detective Svoboda trails the terrors: What if, for instance, Superman's (or her uncle Don's) disguise is actually a "secret" that he held on to for almost sixty years? And that secret spirals out from his Nebraska family back to the American occupation of Japan after the Second World War? What if that occupation occasioned an intricate government cover-up of torture and deaths of U.S. soldiers spanning Tokyo to Washington? And this exemplar of "the Greatest Generation," this Superman, skids and crashes in 2004 because of what he saw, what he perhaps did, as an MP in the Eighth Army stockade in 1946?

"Who tells any war story is what is important," Svoboda observes, "that is, who has the authority to tell it, and then when and why." Her telling of her uncle's war story fashions a nonfiction montage that rivals those of artists like Hannah Höch, Raoul Hausmann, and George Grosz, at once incandescent and devastating. Uncle Don's earnest voice—on the audio tapes he mailed her as she started this book and in the casual notes he wrote home during the war—bumps up against Svoboda's own first-person investigations in archives and libraries, online, and in Nakano streets. Her deflected conversations with her father contend with her candid talks with her son, the lost past versus the ongoing present. Everyone performs multiple, shifting roles—Svoboda's cousin is

Uncle Don's daughter, and his therapist. Svoboda set out believing she was tracking one sort of narrative, then ended up with (and in) another book entirely. "All suicides," she writes, "produce questions about the story of a life. The questions with this one proliferate with all I don't know about his tapes. I thought I was following a tidy coming-of-age account of a young soldier in postwar Japan. Instead there is this mystery of possible executions, with the site of those executions seven thousand miles away."

As Svoboda didn't *choose* this book, her mulishness—and skill—at shadowing her charged materials fall among the vivifying wonders of *Black Glasses Like Clark Kent*. Everywhere she lodges vivid, unexpected particulars—her uncle's revelations about the lice in the "embroidered dragon quilts" he filched from a whorehouse, and the Nebraska settlers "who were driven crazy by the solitude that the Homestead Act had forced them into, pioneering one farm every 160 acres"—even as she stays alert to terminal ambiguity, even failure. Her search shuttles between an obsessive determination to expose every fact, however obscure or tangential, and a clear-eyed recognition of the void. "MPs don't like to keep records," one archivist informs her. "I write to the National Personnel Records for my uncle's official military papers and discover they burned in the great National Archives fire of 1973," she elsewhere admits. Finally, as she concludes, "No document will provide all the details."

The last cassette Svoboda's uncle prepared for her was silent but for an "accidentally" recorded radio news story about Abu Ghraib. *Black Glasses Like Clark Kent* is a book about now as much as then, arcing a continuum of atrocity, race, military justice, censorship, and lies, inventorying the hard legacies of a family, and a nation. "I think he had a deep need to plant a secret he wanted me to find," Svoboda says. "But I grow angry that he's left me such a mystery, and neither the government, nor the archives, nor the guards, nor the relatives have solved it."

We live at a moment when the redemptive (religious) memoir appears to have replaced the therapeutic (family) memoir in the literary marketplace, and even the requisite caveats of resistance to formula epiphanies already sound rote and precious. Polyvocal, oblique, sly, yet fierce, ultimately moral: Svoboda's recounting proves more audacious, although her insistence on seizing the full intractability of her subjects arrives amid a reluctant shrug. "I'll bet you couldn't write a simple story," Svoboda's father teases her over the phone. "I could, I could," she replies, "I just have never found one."

Robert Polito
September 2007

BLACK GLASSES LIKE CLARK KENT

CHAPTER 1

My uncle is Superman. With black Clark Kent glasses, grapefruit-sized biceps, lots of brilliantined thick dark hair, and a solid jaw, six-four and as handsome as all get-out, he's the perfect match for Kryptonite. He even keeps a photo of himself as a high school Adonis, veins bulging. Now, in 2004, after making millions in farming, restaurants, and real estate, instead of swooping down and rescuing people from burning buildings, he volunteers for Meals on Wheels, just what Superman would take on in his advanced years. I suspect this Superman schtick also has something to do with Nietzsche's "will to power." After all, Grandma had more than a whiff of German in her Czech fierceness. *Make the best better* reads the ornately written note I find in her purse after her funeral. My uncle was her baby, he bore a golden sheen that lit his life, made him special, a man with muscle.

A few years ago he tried to convince me that his eighteen months in the army would make a terrific movie, or at least a great book. "I was there during the occupation of Japan, right after World War Two," he said. "They found out we were less barbaric than they were taught. It's quite a story."

I rolled my eyes. Superman had gone too far. I put his confidence down to the vanity of old age, the vanity of somebody who still, at nearly eighty, held himself and his washboard stomach as proudly as any of the Supermen, screen or comic book. But he was adamant, so sure of his story—and of my taking it on as the writer in the family.

"War stories?" I laughed. "Let me tell you how hard it is to get a book published."

"If you're a real Svoboda," he says, "you'll figure out a way. It'll be worth it to you."

It was a beautiful day so I decided to walk several more miles out into the country. I came across a large orchard, perhaps an apple orchard. About a hundred airplanes were hidden underneath the leaf canopy. Most of them looked like they were general aviation planes and some old military planes. They were parked in nice neat rows. I wandered over to several of them. I've always been interested in old planes. They were poorly equipped with what I'd call makeshift armament, kind of old, with little bomb bays crudely cut into them. I never found out if these were general aircraft that people were trying to hide from our bombing or if they were the kamikaze— kind of a last-straw type of thing. The sun was filtering through the leaf canopy and I was the only person there, going from aircraft to aircraft. It felt like the dying of a country, or a giving up. [recorded 01/99]

In spring 2004, reports about Abu Ghraib fill the newspapers; by April the radio talks of nothing else. Especially the kind of radio that everyone in small-town Nebraska listens to, the Rush Limbaugh who rationalizes it all away: "We're going to ruin people's lives over it and we're going to hamper our military effort, and then we are going to really hammer them because they had a good time. . . . I'm talking about people having a good time. These people—you ever heard of emotional release? You ever heard of needing to blow some steam off?"

My dad calls around then and mentions that his brother has fallen into a deep depression. "I think it has

to do with what's going on," he says. "He's got plenty of money, his kids are okay, his wife just bought a new Cadillac. He's never been depressed before."
The psychiatric ward my uncle checks himself into is dead in the center of the country. Only one shrink runs the operation; there are no more psychiatrists for 150 miles. The facility got its start by taking in the settlers who were driven crazy by the solitude that the Homestead Act had forced them into, pioneering one farm every 160 acres. On the fifth of July he calls his daughter Chris and demands to be let out. Maybe he watched all the Fourth of July TV; maybe the military played their pageant music nonstop, surely there were World War II reruns up the kazoo on cable. He tells her he has to get out that very night or else. Chris hears that *or else* better than most—she is a psychologist with her own practice—and suggests he hire a private plane and fly down to Texas where she lives. "He was too close to suicide for antidepressants alone," Chris writes me later. I imagine that, professionally speaking, she hesitates. Perhaps she mentions how slowly antidepressants kick in—sometimes it takes as long as six weeks. But he is her father and nobody else close to him—or anyone else within those 150 miles—will take the professional interest she does. At 3 a.m. July 6, he and his wife hire a plane to fly to Texas. He can't wait for morning.

Years ago, his son Tom tells me this story:
His dad's sixteen and plowing one end of the field. My dad, two years older, plows from the other end. The tractors back then have no air-conditioning, no tape deck, no CD player, no shock absorbers, no cab to keep out the dust or even an umbrella to block a sun that's so hot they've

tied red snot rags over their heads, and the motor thrums as if it will wear the cartilage right off the spine. Sweat drips down their faces as straight as the row after row they make to reach the middle. They grin when they pass each other on the last four of those rows; they bounce so bad they have to grin or lose their teeth. Finally, nose to nose, they shut off their vehicles, carefully set their glasses on the tractor haunches, and jump into the cool dirt clods to wrestle. They grunt and they wrestle, turn after turn, their sweat churning the dirt into mud, until Grandma, with her halo of bottle-bright red hair, hangs over them with a pitcher of lemonade covered with a cloth and a nice *kolache* for each of them. By this time my uncle has my dad's face pushed down into the plowed row beside her and his arm pinned to a broken corn-stalk. But my dad, being older, is still heavier. He flips his brother as soon as he lunges for the lemonade and shoves him down even harder. He calls out, laughing, "Uncle, uncle."

"Why'd you say uncle?" Grandma asks after. "A big boy like you quitting?"

Abu Ghraib, Abu Ghraib. It could have been a Club Med destination it sounded so exotic, so far away. The city near the prison was known for the Abu Ghraib Infant Formula Plant that Western intelligence proclaimed to be a biological weapons production facility. But all they ever found were cans of formula.

CHAPTER 2

I stare at the Get Well rack. What card do you send to a severely depressed person? Although I seldom see my uncle, in New York we take mental health seriously. It is second only to real estate as a topic of discussion. Why, I'm surprised some starving New York artist hasn't put out a line of mental-health cards for at least his fellow artists. In the rest of the country, reports show that over 10 percent of the adult population suffers serious depression annually—probably far more than get married.

Hallmark must be asleep.

A big card with loud colors and a rude joke is what I decide on.

At the end of July I call my uncle. Chris answers. I haven't spoken to her in over thirty years, not since she topped six feet her first year of high school.

"Having him here makes it easier to get him to the appointments," she says. "Thanks so much for the card. He really appreciated it."

"I remember how his arm was hurting him," I say. "He winced when he came to visit Dad in intensive care; he winced and touched that big muscled arm of his and said Mayos had found enough lead in the shattered glass inside to set off a metal detector. He said they couldn't take out the glass."

Thirty years is a lot of silence to break. I'm talking too much and too fast, but it's the only recent two-family story I've got to work with.

"He never complains about his arm," she says. She

smokes or sighs. "He doesn't really believe in psychiatry. Aliens, he would rather believe in, not shrinks, he would sooner tell his troubles to an alien. Maybe a parish priest."

I tell her both my sons take after him in height. "Six-one at fourteen, six-five by twenty." I'm looking at the shoes of my draft-age son. They're taking up half the apartment. I don't want them moved though, I don't want them gone. "Dad was telling me a funny story about your dad, how he had to carry the last three pairs of size-fifteen shoes the army had everywhere he went in Japan. Is that true?"

"He wears a size twelve." She goes quiet. "He doesn't talk about his time in the service."

"He tried to get me to listen to his war stories a couple of years ago," I say.

She makes the sort of nodding sound that only shrinks know how to do, the kind that forces you to go on. But what do I have to go on with? Her dad and I never got around to talking.

"They sure aren't treating them so well in Iraq," I say. I expect a squawk—she lives in the reddest state there is—but she just says it's a bad thing. In the next long pause, I decide maybe she needs cheering up herself. "Remember those wild kittens we found in the washhouse at Grandma's—do you keep a cat now?"

"I barely have time to keep a husband." Then she's telling me her dad will be back in an hour, and he'll tell me himself how much he liked the card.

"I thought he'd like it," I say quickly. "Grandma would never have approved."

O Superman, sings Laurie Anderson.

. . .

We quickly found out what the four hundred eighty-third MPEG did. The EG *behind the* MP *letters stood for "escort guard." That meant we went about anywhere, and did about anything. The cabaret I guarded in Tokyo was about ninety-five percent black because of the camp nearby. The black soldiers were in the quartermaster and the supply end of the army. A few white sailors would come in on the ships. One night a couple of them came in, acting like they were still in San Diego. They started dancing with some of the girls that the blacks kind of thought they owned because during the day they lived with the black soldiers in their tents. One of the sailors and a black man got into an argument. The black man took out a knife and before I could get over there, he took a swing at the guy's throat. He missed but when the sailor put his hand up, the soldier cut off his thumb.*

I thought the best course was to get the hell out of there so I grabbed the sailor. I knew we couldn't go down this long hallway because blacks were lined up on both sides so I went for the men's restroom. Toilets in Japan are just flat to the floor. These were in front of the windows. I took the sailor and pushed him over this toilet and out the window. There was about a six-foot drop. I followed him, running across the big paved lot that was an old bombed-out warehouse. The blacks started coming out the door, and two of them got their trucks and tried to run us down out in this big area. Fortunately there were some poles we could hide behind, and we finally got across the street and into a big concrete structure that was a baseball stadium I had never paid much attention to. We ran up the stairs and hid.

The people in charge of the system didn't know what

*the real world was like, putting white MPs in charge of
black soldiers.* [recorded 01/99]

By 1946 the Eighth Army in Japan reported that "racial
agitation" between black and white troops was the primary cause of assault, the most frequent violent crime
among the American troops stationed there.

"'Where's the giant?' all the little Nip kids asked when
they saw those huge shoes of his outside their paper
doors," says my dad.

We're parked in a small-town Safeway lot. I'm visiting
Nebraska from New York. We have all our most impor-
tant conversations at Safeway while the ice cream melts.
It's still July, it's melting.

"Uncle Don is tall," I say. "The Japanese were really
short then, they didn't have much to eat."

Dad punches on the AC. "Why didn't the two of you
work on that book about his war stories a couple of
years ago?"

I watch two women claim the same grocery cart. "I
told him to put them on tape for me so I could get an
idea about what should be done with them. Then I never
heard from him again."

"You discouraged him."

"I was only being realistic. Somebody has to record the stories to get them down. He could do that for
himself."

"It's hard to do things when you're depressed." Dad
sets his jaw as if even saying *depressed* in this part of the
world is dangerous.

"He wasn't depressed then. And why doesn't he
try to get a writer to work with him who at least lives
nearby?"

Dad gives me his appraising look, a sidelong glance. "He likes you."

I don't say that my uncle's hardly ever spoken to me personally before, let alone called me back. I'm the eldest of nine children and have always been addressed as part of the herd. Despite my uncle's involving Dad in his many convoluted business schemes, we've been strictly wedding-invitation relatives; we have never even eaten turkey together. My mother and his wife—something didn't work. "All relatives like a writer," I say. "They think we will make them immortal by writing their life story."

He laughs. "I never asked you."

"You might," I say.

He purses his lips, annoyed with me. "I think it would help him to write up his story," he says. "If it's a good one, I'll let you do mine."

"Women do the wash, cook the food, explain everybody's feelings, and write the book."

"Hey," he says, "maybe you could get a movie deal out of it. It'll be your big break."

"A story about a kid who's a military policeman in Japan?"

He taps on his window. "Once I thought I heard you say any story sells, as long as it's told right."

I stare at the summer bugs writhing on the windshield. What am I really going to get out of this other than *You've got it wrong*? "I don't remember him talking about his war stories growing up. Why is he so interested suddenly in telling them now?"

Dad rubs his old eyes under his glasses. His time in intensive care was just last year. He clears his throat. "He has a secret," he says.

CHAPTER 3

Twice Dad besieged his draft board with letters, begging them to draft him before the war was over. His father had a severe case of diabetes, and he and his brother were supposed to keep the farm going. "You couldn't imagine the peer pressure," says Dad. "My brother must've written the same letters. And he was in love with the girl next door."

No doubt the free education promised after just eighteen months of service contributed to their parents' agreeing to let them go. After all, the boys worked at the farm only in the summer. They did the spring plowing and fall harvest on weekends, driving five hours across the state to where their father had finagled cheap land during the Depression. The plan was that they would get hired men to take their places with the money they made in the service. Besides, everyone was sure the war would be finished any day now, and all the casualties were over. At least that must've been how the two lovers saw it.

My uncle's girlfriend was just fifteen. At the end of the war her father was serving in Iran, keeping the oil-supply lines open. Her mother worked as a legal secretary. Back then, my uncle's wife-to-be looked very much like Lauren Bacall. At least five-eleven, blonde and slim, she was obviously worth keeping in touch with, and he did: he sent her letters every few weeks. Garrulous on paper, he must have been quite the fast talker in person.

He also had a roving eye.

His parents were at the farm and my dad was already stationed in the Philippines when he received his orders. His sister was supposed to look out for him—he was barely eighteen—but she resented his going because he would no longer be around to bring his buddies home for her. She left a note on the table telling him to be sure to take all his dirty laundry.

Her name was Kyochan.

We'd walk around the little park there and sit on a cold bench while I tried to learn Japanese and she tried to improve her English. It got so we were holding each other and squeezing—the Japanese don't believe in kissing. Taboo, I guess. Anyway, they have other ways of indicating amorous intentions. It was obvious the friendship was turning into something a little more than amorous. Eventually after we walked to the front gate and said good-bye, we made a commitment to meet each other in the park. I didn't have duty that time of day. The park was about a block away and we sat on the bench there and got a little more amorous. I had a friend who was doing guard duty that night so we could just walk into the compound. I didn't want to take her to where my barracks was because probably fifty people slept there so we walked around the back of the building where it was cold and the snow was still sifting down. Then we found the boiler room where it was warm and very inviting. We climbed up on a scaffold that had a platform over this boiler and did the natural thing. It was extremely enjoyable.

Our biggest trouble was finding a place to go. At that time, it seemed like everything important happened in the boiler room. [recorded 01/99]

"Our biggest trouble was finding a place to go."

"They keep trying to get me to stop all this Madam Butterflying around," General Douglas MacArthur told Major Faubion Bowers shortly after they arrived in Japan. "I won't do it. My father told me never to give an order unless I was certain it would be carried out. I wouldn't issue a no-fraternization order for all the tea in China."

At eighteen, my uncle wasn't a whit naïve about women:

We were in a real nice whorehouse where they had quilts on the beds with beautifully embroidered dragons. We were checking their cards and the girls were very playful. They'd come up behind us and whack us with a pillow on the head. They were just kids. This other MP with me, we got fond of these two beds with the embroidered dragon quilts on them so we grabbed the quilts and threw them out the window—this was on the second floor—and hopped down the stairs and collected them. The girls came after us but we made it back to the silk mill with our quilts and put them on our beds. They looked pretty snappy. Everybody pays the price and about three weeks later we had a bad case of lice. [recorded 03/99]

Two weeks into the occupation, the Japanese newspapers reported a rising number of criminal acts by GIs. Of course, stealing bedspreads is not much of a criminal act, but an atmosphere of lawlessness prevailed. MacArthur promptly ordered the newspapers silenced. He didn't want bad publicity to undermine his job of getting the Japanese to buy into democracy. Besides, bad publicity back home might hurt his chances for the presidency. To learn about what was really going on in postwar Japan, there are only the GIs' letters home, and the reports— often years later—by the occupied Japanese themselves.

The soldiers in Iraq let us know what's going on with their blogs and cell-phone pictures. It was an MP named Joseph Darby who anonymously passed criminal investigators a CD-ROM full of prison photos from Abu Ghraib.

CHAPTER 4

MPs are big galoots in white gloves who break up fights in bars and drag drunk GIs back to their barracks. That's about all most people think they do. But MPs also direct traffic, support the local police, confiscate weapons, guard buildings, make up honor guards and, in my uncle's case, check out brothels, and guard prisons. In an occupation, MPs carry guns, but they're mostly impotent. They are supposed to enforce the peace, not antagonize it. But they are surrounded by people whose relatives have been killed by the occupiers. Whom to trust is always a problem. Without knowing the language or customs, they become isolated and defensive. Standing between the occupied and the occupiers, MPs are always in the position of being threatened or humiliated—or bored.

Recruited for size and primitive persuasive skills, MPs would rather fight than guard. Especially my uncle, who loved to fight and fought three-minute bouts on the boat over. He became an MP by virtue of being more than six feet tall and "not too skinny." He had no training. Many months after he served, recruits completed a six-week course that taught them the proper way to deal with prisoners, handle their weapons, and maintain a professional distance from the inmates and the locals. But in the postwar chaos, my uncle had to figure it all out for himself.

In Iraq MPs are supposed to "set the conditions" with "enhanced interrogation techniques," as the radio puts it.

It features Abu Ghraib months after those MPs—and the
military contractors—were caught. Young MPs, perhaps
sadistic, surely stupid, definitely frustrated by a lack of
opportunity at home and militarily in combat, did what
they were told to do. But there will always be an MP who
has to watch while the other MPs work, and one of those
will tell on the others.
Until then, nothing happens, nobody is hurt.

In Japan, the MPs picked on each other:

*One night we came in after a big drinking bout, and we
found the old vets all zipped up in their sleeping bags—
we called them fart sacks—with just their heads sticking
out. We opened the windows and grabbed them by the
zipper and pitched them out into the snow. Fortunately
there was about five or six foot of snow on the ground.
We should have been shot but we weren't.* [recorded
01/99]

It's 1969. I'm my uncle's age when he became an MP. I
shake my fist outside the White House at 2 a.m., marching
with all the other braless and hairy eighteen- to twenty-
year-olds. Although one boy from my high school has
died in Vietnam, not one of my boyfriends has—but they
do have draft numbers that make them nervous, so nervous they cook up plans to hide, to flee, get sick, maim
themselves. Together we scream our slogans as loudly as
we can, as if all our noise will actually change LBJ's mind.
The searchlights on the White House lawn are blinding;
we can hardly see the black O mouths of the tank muzzles
pointed at us, but the soldiers' silhouettes are sharp. The
first faces I see when the sun comes up, the first soldiers I
pay for with taxes from my first summer job that actually

makes decent money, are of boys my age, and they are pointing their guns at me. My niece tells me that over half her graduating class of 2004, both boys and girls, plan to serve in Iraq. I hear this from her in my father's kitchen, over the Fox News broadcast blaring war news from his bedroom. I'm not surprised. My hometown is surrounded by counties designated "poorest in the United States," with per capita incomes of just over six thousand dollars, according to Thomas Frank's *What's the Matter with Kansas? How Conservatives Won the Heart of America*. The Deep Midwest, not the Deep South, is where extreme poverty meets extreme Republicanism. To our high school graduates, promises of college money go a long way—it's the perfect place for recruiting.

Why do I hesitate to call my uncle again? He is my favorite relative. It's like talking to Dad, only he flirts more, cracks jokes, and does not always say "fine" when you ask how he is. His illness must be serious because nobody ever admits to being depressed in our family; nobody admits feeling anything positive or negative, and never publicly. *Snap out of it* is the mantra. *Don't spend time, work it to death* was another of Grandma's maxims.

Svoboda means "freedom" in Czech. The Czech Republic has a problem with freedom; it's a country without natural borders that's always being overrun. Most recently, the Communists controlled it. The English prime minister Neville Chamberlain handed the country over to Hitler in World War II. The Hapsburgs did the same thing seventy years earlier, with Hungary. To stay free— *Svoboda!*—Czechs have to be crafty and hard working.

My uncle teases boys who aren't manly enough, he makes fun of my brother who is epileptic and dyslexic and suffers nosebleeds. He makes fun of my second brother who can't plant fast enough, who doesn't lift weights. He makes fun of my third brother who has taken up painting. He doesn't make fun of my last brother because he is severely retarded and can't talk, hardly even walks. Too easy.

My own boys don't play sports. They should be good at basketball with height like his kids, or at least at football, the blood in their veins being from Nebraska, a state that falls so silent on September Saturdays you can hear the game on the streets without turning on your TV. "Those boys of yours should use those long arms for something useful," my uncle said the last time they met.

I'm not sure why he teases. His own sons are built of steel and have minds that chew and lock on difficulty with brilliance. Tom is a terrific golf-playing, Mensa-member farmer; Mike was named Farmer of the Year while he was still in his twenties. My uncle keeps them close to the earth; he buys his boys farms that they, the supersons of Superman, turn into model farms. Teasing's not his only show of affection—he's a big hugger, a bigger hugger than Dad. Surely he teased his daughter. Did his mother, the redhead who had a halo of white hair when I knew her—Saint Grandma—did she train him to tease by teasing him? She cheated every time she played cards with us, her own grandchildren. She would pick a better hand, change the rules. Or is this teasing some third-generation-pioneer testing, the torture that makes you tough enough? *Svoboda!*

I had a really tough sergeant. I thought he was a pretty nasty person, although all he wanted to do was make good soldiers out of us in those short four and a half months [of boot camp], which was kind of an impossibility. I had made the boxing team and he didn't like that type of activity. He'd march us out of camp ten or fifteen miles and then turn to me and say, "You can go out for boxing now." It would be three or four in the afternoon and I had to be at practice by five. I'd have to run back through the woods over these streams. I didn't realize that the tougher he was, the better the chances of my survival if I were ever unfortunate enough to get into real combat. [recorded 01/99]

Everyone fought in the forties. Wartime meant fight time, proving manhood in combat as well as sport. Back then, boxing matches made front-page headlines; they played blow-by-blow on the radio; people staged fistfights in empty lots; even my scrawny ten-year-old mother boxed the neighbor boys to win money for her brothers.

Dad tells me he and his brother drove his parents down to Corpus Christi one summer when they were teenagers. His dad had just finished a treatment for diabetes—primarily of vinegar, the way Dad remembers it. The two boys took off for a local dance hall, his brother, fifteen, looking about twelve with that baby face of his. But not, of course, with all his muscles pumped from lifting weights.

First off, his brother finds a sailor to fight. Dad is a little distracted by the girls, all the long black hair and dark eyes, the kind my mother has, so he doesn't follow the two of them outside. It is none of his business anyway—he's not a fighter. When his brother comes back in, he pulls Dad off the dance floor and says to him, "I think I killed him." "What?" Dad shouts over the loud band. His brother throws a few punches and a kayo. Before Dad can figure out what is going on, the sailor staggers back into the dance hall, his nose bleeding and his shirt ripped, and he walks right up and shakes hands with his brother. "What a helluva good fight that was," he says. He wears the indentation of a class ring smack in the middle of his forehead.

They tried to get me to put the gloves on with a big guy called "Indian," who was a full-blooded Indian, a big burly sullen guy. Fortunately, I evaded the issue. Four stops from where we were stationed there was a kodokan, *the main meetinghouse for people interested in judo. I decided right then and there I was going to get a black belt.* [recorded 03/99]

The film *From Here to Eternity,* released in 1953, was based on a book by James Jones. Like Jones, my uncle qualified for a Golden Gloves tournament after the war, but they didn't have anyone in his weight class in town, so he didn't compete. In the film, Burt Lancaster plays the boxer-turned-soldier, and when he refuses to join the boxing squad, he is warned: "You put your head in a noose." Ernest Borgnine, playing the stockade commander, nearly beats Frank Sinatra to death in the brig for insulting him. Even a man "good with his hands" like Burt Lancaster is helpless to protect him when faced with the unlimited power of the stockade's commander.

CHAPTER 5

My uncle and his daughter decide on electroshock treatment. It's had very good results with patients over seventy. They have already CAT-scanned his whole body twice, and she has had every imaginable specialist in central Texas examine him. He's added severe eye pain to his depression problem, yet still no one can find anything physically wrong with him. Chris manages to allay his fear of becoming "a refried bean" as a result of the electroshock. To him, it falls into the same category of extreme medicine as lobotomy, a procedure hyped in the 1950s to cure everything from facial warts to hydrocephalus. My own brother, severely epileptic, barely escaped it. But electroshock isn't supposed to be the electric chair anymore where you bite down on a tongue depressor and scream while your body writhes in the restraints. Its application is supposed to relieve whatever deep is bothering you so that the shock is forgotten.

In his essay "The Remorse of the Heart," the German writer W. G. Sebald focuses on the forgetting of the Holocaust: the way it exiles the forgetters from history and ruins a society that "misplaces" its torture and murder. Like Freud, he believes forgetting looks accidental but is really a structured activity.

Dad says this spring his brother came over to him in the little two-entrée café where they always have lunch, told him he was depressed, and said he hoped it would never happen to him. "It was invisible, he was walking and talking the way he always did," Dad says. He told him he was sorry to hear that and finished his lunch.

Our new home was in an old silk textile mill in Yokohama's industrial area. It was easy to identify from a distance, having a ziggety-zaggety roofline designed to let in more light. We had orientation in a big room surrounded by silk-weaving machines. You got a good view of the city when it looked just like a prairie strewn with house foundations. Our first assignment was to guard and keep secure a large barbed-wire-enclosed prison of about two hundred fifty prisoners thirty miles away. The first night of guarding I climbed one of the towers. They were wooden and about twenty feet high. This one had a sliding door and because of all the rain, it was sticking open. In order to keep warm, soldiers would take a steel helmet with a piece of cloth in it and our gas and light it. Like a good soldier, I got sleepy and slept for maybe a half an hour. I was chilly when I woke. Cold—you know. I grabbed the five-gallon can of gas and poured it right into the cloth of the helmet. There were still ashes there and the gasoline blew up. I dove through the door and on the way down I caught my foot on one of the power lines, which then fell on my head and knocked me unconscious. I landed in a pool of water about a foot deep, face down. One of the prisoners saved me. He was coming to cook breakfast and dragged me out of the pond and called an ambulance.

I was unconscious for two days. I had a concussion and got quite a few stitches in my left arm where I pushed through the glass window. The hospital was really a schoolhouse with school still going on. It was the darndest thing, our hospital beds in the halls and

*little Japanese kids walking by and looking down at
you. For recreation we had some benches out in the
courtyard, and they projected movies against the wall of
the school. After about a week, I had had enough and
put my clothes on and walked out.
I just couldn't remember which military police outfit
I was in.* [recorded 03/99]

Chris has seen other old men get through this treatment, open their eyes, and say *Great, I feel great.* But the
electroshock doesn't work very well and now my uncle
won't wait for doctors' appointments. Chris has to pull
in all her favors to make sure the doctors are poised to
receive him the minute the two of them walk into the
waiting room or he stomps out, frantic in his pain. The
drugs don't work very well either and then he stops taking them, telling her that he doesn't want to become an
addict.

There is no changing his mind.

The famed biographer Janet Malcolm writes that, while
everyone believes fiction, everyone questions nonfiction.
Facts are always questionable. Memory is porous, condi-
tional with regard to the weather, the audience, the time
of day, a slant of light. The power of the imagination in
fiction is that it sees so clearly; it so easily prunes the in-
essential away to pure truth.

Maybe it's an advantage that I don't know my uncle well.
The outline of his story will remain stark, his actions
meaningful and uncomplicated by nuance, and my imagination will have to be summoned to make it cohere.

And he wants to tell me the story.

He wants to tell it, even though there's a history of

estrangement between both our families—or is it just silence? They always say they're coming over, but they seldom do. We'll see them at the grocery store or the feedlot and they're always glad to see us. Is it their dad's secret that makes them cautious? Do they know my dad knows it?

At least I knew I was in the military police. I decided I'd go to the train station in Tokyo and take every train out for about ten stations because I knew one of the trains ran right behind the silk mill and I would recognize the building with the ziggety-zaggety roof.

The train station looked like the Coliseum in Rome. It was bombed out and didn't have a roof. The first day I rode the trains for about ten hours and wasn't at all successful. I started to doubt myself how many stops we were out of Tokyo and became discouraged. I also didn't have any place to sleep. When darkness came, I went into a Japanese house and found the mom and dad asleep on the floor. They had the only bed. I just scooched the man over and laid down and slept. There was a lot of mumbling and talking fast Japanese but it didn't bother me any. In the morning, they cooked breakfast for me.

I began to get tired of riding the trains. That night I found another group of soldiers camped in the main part of Tokyo and mooched a meal from them and slept in the boiler room. It was a very cold night. I was really getting discouraged. Besides, it was Christmas Eve. Being lost in a big city like Tokyo, not being able to speak the language, not knowing where you were supposed to go—it was a scary experience. I boarded trains again the next day. After about ten stops out on the second train I took, I was ready to get off and quit, when

"Being lost in a big city like Tokyo ..."

I decided to ride just two more stations. There was the ziggety-zaggety roof. [recorded 03/99]

I fly from New York to Nebraska again to stage my dad's surprise eightieth-birthday party. My hands, up to their wrists in raw meat and ketchup, are making a meat loaf I plan to disguise as a birthday cake because he can't have sugar.

"You haven't reached my brother yet," says Dad.

"No," I say, "not yet. I have a lot going on—I haven't finished my last project, I'm still teaching, we're selling the house. What is it with his war stories and you?" I crack the egg into the bowl, then work the yolk into the meat with my hands. "Really," I say.

My father is eating a pear with a touch of ketchup. Having diabetes makes him liable to try anything. He shrugs. "I told you I couldn't tell you," he says.

"Give me a break," I say. "Something to do with the war, of course."

He's already chopped the onions and peppers. He scrapes them into a well in the middle of the meat, then adds a handful of papery oatmeal and a big can of slimy tomatoes.

"Maybe my brother's driven by this secret and that's what's making him so depressed."

I shape the meat into a loaf pan. I wait for him to

tell me more. But I am not the most patient person. Two beats later, I say, "What does he have to do now that he's transferred title to everything he owns to his kids? He must be bored—bacon, please."

"He'll never be bored," he says. He peels several strips of bacon from the frozen supply and hands them to me. I lay them across the top of the loaf. "He'd take up skydiving before he got bored."

"And if I got him to tape his stories, wouldn't that make him more depressed? What if he can't remember things? Or he remembers the wrong things?"

Dad shrugs. "I don't think you can get more depressed than he is now."

"Do we have candles?" I say while I wash my hands. Bits of raw meat mix with the soap on the way down the drain.

Dad is wedging the rest of the bacon back into the freezer. "Ask your sister for candles; why would I have candles?"

"Mom never throws anything out, for one thing." I wipe my hands on the dish towel. "Is this secret something you just cooked up? Just how long have you known about this?"

"I'll be eighty tomorrow, in case you've forgotten."

I hide my smile.

He toys with the sugar in the sugar bowl. "It's been about sixty years."

CHAPTER 6

One very bitter day, I couldn't take the cold anymore and stepped inside the guardhouse. A jeep buzzed through at about twenty miles an hour. I jumped off my chair and made the jeep back up. The man inside popped out. "Young man, what if I just kept on driving, we'd have lost a vehicle. What would you do?"

"I'd shoot you in the back of the head," I said.

He looked at me for about thirty seconds and then put the car in gear and drove off. He was a colonel and had already checked out the vehicle. He was just checking the security. He realized I was serious about my job and didn't say anything about sitting inside the building after that. [recorded 03/99]

"Killing is what war is all about, and killing in combat, by its very nature, causes deep wounds of pain and guilt," writes Lieutenant Colonel David Grossman in his book *On Killing: The Psychological Cost of Learning to Kill in War and Society.* As a member of the military, he wants to find out how to turn the killing on and off rather than to eliminate it. The psychological aftermath he sees is seen as the major stumbling block. "The dead soldier takes his misery with him, but the man who killed him must forever live and die with him," writes Grossman.

My uncle served after a war, after all the killing, during an occupation.

. . .

Dad spanked me when I was small. Sometimes it was just because I was the eldest, to provide an example, sometimes I was set up by my brother. He punched and left no marks; my sister and I clawed and left scars. Often we were all spanked, no matter whose fault it was. The spanking "settled us down."

Most people believe that punishment is good, it's what keeps people from repeatedly doing bad things. Of course, this has been proven wrong. Many people agree that isolating the individual who does wrong is also a good idea. Stand in the corner. Get those fists out of range. Solitary? This has been proven to cause insanity and blindness. Give those fists something better to do—that's been proven right. Weave those baskets, stamp those plates. But a stockade is where prisoners are held, not rehabilitated.

MPs are not supposed to inflict punishment anymore, they are only supposed to make certain that people conform to the rules. But punishment is the first and simplest tool of enforcement, the cornerstone of military justice, which is distinctly not civilian justice. As a June 1946 investigation by the House of Representatives' Committee on Military Affairs stated:

> Many lawyers and others entering the Army
> from civil life with ideas of justice based on
> the ancient Anglo-Saxon respect for the rights
> of the individual, find themselves shocked by
> disregard for these rights in the Army's military
> justice, and hundreds of thousands, probably mil-
> lions, of plain soldiers are contemptuous or bitter
> about it.

The real question is, how far should such punishment go, for both imprisoned military and enemy prisoners. The debate rages in the United States now, especially regarding the extrajudicial detention of Guantánamo prisoners guarded by MPs and hired contractors, where punishment-turned-torture is expected to reveal secrets obtained no other way.

Punishment for the mere fact of race is always harsher than any other. Race can't be helped. Nips, spics—what did the Germans call everyone else? They are always the Other, after all. Not your brother.

Twenty out of the twenty-one reported executions in the Pacific during the war were of black soldiers.

My uncle always shouts into the telephone as if it can't quite carry his voice all that way, and he shouts louder if he's calling long-distance. He's not hard of hearing—that's how he learned to use the telephone in the days of the party line. I find myself doing the same thing on a cell phone. How can those tiny little holes not even facing my mouth pick up what I'm saying?

The quiet after his loud *Hello* is stunning. I forget how I was going to beg him to tell me his stories because Dad thinks it will make him feel better; I just say, "So where are all your stories about Japan?"—blunt and simple, no small talk. "Why haven't you sent them to me?"

"I was at the store," he says, "buying batteries."

He can still make a joke. "For four years?"

"I thought you'd forgotten all about my army career," he says. "But I did make a few tapes like you suggested."

"That's what Dad said," I say. "That's good news."

"I could do the rest of the tapes, I suppose," he says. "I have the time."

There's a beat where I imagine all the time he has, being so depressed. I wonder whether he'll tell me why he's so depressed in the tapes, or maybe even tell me his secret. "Mail me whatever you have finished so I can get them transcribed," I say. "That way I can see what we've got to work with." Then, although money isn't something that's supposed to come between relatives—it's worse than between friends—I picture myself bent over the typewriter, headphones tight against my ears, listening to the clearing of his throat, the tedium of one meandering anecdote after another, all the while thinking of all the other work I have to do, and I say, "I should send out the tapes to get a good transcription. That might cost as much as five hundred dollars. Would you pay for that?"

"I thought you'd just type it all up into a book."

"I'm more of a writer than a typist," I say. "It takes a lot of work to get a book ready. My first novel took fifteen years. Then you have to convince someone that the book's good enough to publish. That takes time too."

"I suppose it is a speculative business," he says. "I know a little about that from farming."

"Serious writing," I go on, warming up, "is a sort of obsession. Money comes second. Anyway, I don't usually work with tapes. I'll need them transcribed, and that costs money."

There's a pause. "Five hundred will be fine," he says. "Send me the bill. Just remember me when you get the advance for the movie."

I can't tell if he's teasing. "We'll write it in the contract," I say in my sternest voice.

He laughs. "I'll mail you all the tapes I've made already. I left the first one in a drawer in a house that I'm selling, but I'll stop the closing tomorrow and fetch it."

"That's serious," I say. I'm surprised by his swift response, the call to action. "I'd appreciate it," I go on, the way I'm supposed to.

Now what? I can't just hang up. I could ask how hot it is, but that's way too lame. I can't ask how he's feeling.

I ask anyway.

"Terrible," he says. "Not so good."

"And how's the weather?" I say like he's just said *fine.*

"Texas," he says, "is like hell with the lid left on."

"Nice," I say. "I am really looking forward to the tapes."

CHAPTER 7

The Eighth Army stockade included the South Pacific, the Philippine Islands, and all the islands throughout that area. The powers that be requisitioned the main prison of Tokyo for all these prisoners. Myself and three other MPs were assigned to go out and clean it up. We loaded up what we thought were the necessary supplies, including about six cases of beer, and headed out for this city called Nakano, about twenty miles from Tokyo. There were no guards and the main gate was open. A few Japanese prisoners wandered aimlessly inside. They were left when the Japanese pulled out and wore prison uniforms. They acted very happy to see us.

For ourselves, we chose a couple of rooms in the administration building about three stories off the ground. No officer came with us so we decided to stay up and drink beer and play cards until four in the morning. Around six o'clock we woke up to hear a loud humming noise, the sound of hundreds of voices. The whole courtyard in front of the prison was full of Japanese. Knowing that the U.S. had taken over, they had all come to the prison, looking for work.

We picked about forty of them to be our workforce for the next couple of weeks. Later we found out we had to body-search them every time they left and decided we would have

"... we would have been better off picking some younger, prettier girls."

been better off picking some of the younger, prettier girls.
[recorded 08/04]

Military prisons are of two types: penal, for punishing
and attempting to reform criminals within the military;
and confinement-oriented, where captured enemies are
confined for military reasons until hostilities cease.

The Eighth Army stockade was of the first type. Ten
acres in total, with nine guardhouses, it was the largest
stockade in all of Asia. Eighteen- to twenty-year-old boys
guarded veterans with medals from all the terrible battle-
fields of the Pacific, as well as boys their own age who
could not resist the temptations of the occupation. They
were just waiting to be shipped out to serve their sentences at Fort Leavenworth or another stateside prison.
But their ride home was not top priority.

Sugamo Prison, three miles away, was the second
type of prison, where Tojo, Japan's prime minister, and
seventy-seven other Japanese prisoners were finally executed. Twenty-year-olds ran that prison too; Chuck Mayne
was barely twenty when he took the job.

Abu Ghraib is the contemporary version of Sugamo.
The largest prison in Iraq, it is located about twenty kilo-
meters west of Baghdad and covers 280 acres. The prison
grounds contain five different compounds, each of which
is secured by high walls and guard towers. Although
every large base contains a lock-up for GIs under arrest,
I could never find out whether Abu Ghraib also held our
soldiers at the time of the scandal.

"The occupation of Japan had great moral and legal le-
gitimacy in the eyes of everyone—the American people,
the victorious Allied powers, Japan's Asian neighbors,"
according to John W. Dower, author of the Pulitzer Prize–

winning *Embracing Defeat: Japan in the Wake of World War II.* "There was not a single incident of terrorism against U.S. forces there after World War II."

The soldiers in Tokyo were given pink cards printed with "Where is the bar?" in phonetically spelled-out Japanese. Price lists for the whorehouses were posted on the quartermaster bulletin boards in all U.S. Army camps:

> 20 yen—a buck and a quarter—for the first hour, 10 yen for each additional hour, and all night for 50 yen. If you pay more, you spoil it for all the rest. The MPs will be stationed at the doors to enforce these prices. Trucks will leave here each hour, on the hour. NO MATTER HOW GOOD IT FEELS WITHOUT ONE, BE SURE TO WEAR ONE.

My uncle suffers a minor stroke during electroshock and decides to give it up. He starts losing weight. His eyes begin to hurt him so much that Chris telephones a retinologist at ten o'clock on a Sunday morning and asks him to make a house call. She is so persuasive that the specialist actually drives over and examines him in their living room. But he finds nothing. Perhaps the pain is psychosomatic? Her father is not interested in this diagnosis.

Three years ago my uncle's grandson killed two people. It was dawn the night after his twenty-first birthday party; he was driving fast down a country road, and he hit another truck. A father and son, driving to their farm. The light of the sun or the truck lights shone in his grandson's eyes; he tried to stop but he was too late. He served a

year of community service in his college town, picking
up trash; he went back to school.

A year later, at a construction site, he stepped on a
plank full of nails, which struck him in the face and put
out his eye. He had to lie on a couch perfectly still for five
hours with a nail in his eye until a specialist was found to
stabilize it. Five hours with a nail stuck in his eye.

Death and eye pain. Coincidence. The word "coincidence" comes from the Latin, *co-*, meaning "with," and
incidere, "to fall on."

CHAPTER 8

Each cell was just big enough to put an army cot in and to walk around one side—very minimal. There wasn't any running water or toilet facilities. The walls were about twenty-five feet high with guard towers every ten feet or so, about a mile around. It was a huge place. Inside the wall were several demolished buildings, which proved to be a good spot to put prisoners to pulverize the rock. Eventually it held about six hundred prisoners, half of them in there for the death sentence, the other half for six months. The army didn't seem to believe in anything in between. It was six months or death.

Towards summer, about two or three hours a day, we would take the prisoners out of their cells and we would conduct an exercise period, including a close-order drill where you'd do the march and then the cadence and the about-face, left, right sort of thing. It was really halfway enjoyable because the prisoners were black people and they had songs they'd sing and march to the cadence that they'd jive or drag their legs through. [recorded 09/04]

"Nowhere in these postwar documents is there even the shadow of a suspicion that segregation itself might have played a role in creating a racial disparity in sentencing. No one, as yet, was willing to venture the obvious: it was patently absurd that 8.5 percent of the armed forces could be responsible for committing 79 percent of all capital crimes," wrote Alice Kaplan in *The Interpreter*, a recent book about the difference in sentencing for white and black soldiers accused of the same crime in the European theater of World War II.

Alvin "Tommy" Bridges, an MP during the war and a future police chief, recounted his memories of "military justice" to Studs Terkel in *The Good War.* "They shot some of those guys up there that were—if you'd go to a municipal court, they'd dismiss the case. Depending a lot upon the commanding officer."

The Eighth Army stockade held an almost equal number of blacks and whites, but the most serious offenders were predominantly black.

"Did you ever see a black person before you went into the army?"

Dad says plenty. "They went to Lincoln High. They were all right, a little rough sometimes. In the Philippines they drove the trucks."

As the summer wears on, Chris and her father visit all the museums in the area, the big ones full of art, both abstract and cowboy, and the tiny ones in small towns exhibiting just a few cards of labeled barbed wire under glass. He travels to any museum she can find and spends hours reviewing the exhibition. "I like to see it all gathered together," he tells her. His wife isn't quite so keen on museum trips. She stays home and does other things. No doubt she needs to relax. It can't be easy having a suicidal husband around all day. A lovely woman, still very Lauren Bacall, she has always played his equal but far surpasses him in the area of patience. After he gives up on the electroshock, they move out of Chris's house and rent another, a two-bedroom on a creek not far from Austin. They still see each other daily.

Chris quits her job and farms out her patients. How

does it feel to have your own father under your care? It is one thing to nick one's father's artery in heart surgery and quite another to ask the wrong question, to set him off into silence. He sits in silence all day if they don't go to a museum, a man who couldn't sit still all his life, he sits. His sitting accuses her. It is her fault he is depressed. After all, she is the shrink. She tells him she is not his shrink, it is not ethical, plainly not a good idea. But he won't have it any other way. She is the Mayo Clinic of shrinks, trust is what the relationship is all about; and she's his kin, the stuff of Greek tragedy. All this running around to museums is why he's losing weight. But why does he want to read every caption if his eyes hurt so much? What is he trying to see? What has he seen?

My finger was just banging up against the trigger, you know, nervous. We looked into each other's eyes about a foot apart. He had the damndest eyes. They were kind of—where the light was supposed to be, they were kind of yellow. He was just an evil man. We stared at each other and I finally stared him down. [recorded 08/04]

There's been a 38 percent decline in the number of new black recruits going to Iraq. The men don't see why they should kill other people of color to make corporations richer. Black soldiers in World War II felt a similar hesitation killing Japanese men even though propaganda screened corporate involvement better then—and, of course, the Japanese attacked Pearl Harbor.

   The official line for what the soldiers were doing during the occupation is best illustrated by a quote from the *Soldiers Guide to Japan,* published by the U.S. Army in 1946: "Instead of widespread raping, looting, and pillage, [the Japanese] witnessed GIs giving their kids chewing gum."

. . .

"I'll bet you couldn't write a simple story," says Dad on the phone.

"I could, I could. I just have never found one." I am doing dishes, the receiver in the crook of my shoulder.

Dad is disgusted with me. He says I need a really good plot and that would make all the difference. "Just wait until you hear all my brother's story. Too bad he didn't send the tapes express."

"He's only got one story?" I say. "That'll be a relief." I rinse the spaghetti pot. "Tell me about the time you cooked meat loaf for four hundred GIs and turned the heat up to get it done and burnt the pans right off."

"His stories all lead to something," he says.

"A secret?" I say.

"He's a helluva storyteller," says Dad, dodging my bait. "Maybe that's where you got your talent."

"Not from you?" I say. "I thought you liked to take all the credit."

"For these complicated, tortured little stories of yours? You should've gone into real estate. You would be good at that. Land, that's what I'm good at."

I watch my son open the fridge, remove a chicken thigh, then a breast, then a leg. "That's dinner," I say off the phone, but he's gone. I shove the fridge closed. "You know plenty," I say to Dad. "You used to be a lawyer and a judge. This farming thing is just a ruse to get outdoors."

"I did develop an interest in the truth, that's right, and that led me straight back to farming." He chuckles.

"You're the farmer from Chekhov, one of his bourgeois rich peasants with all the daughters."

"Now those were stories," says Dad. "Those were simple."

CHAPTER 9

My uncle has already sold his three-thousand-acre farm, the airplane he flew to survey his acreage, his shopping center and restaurant and sundry other holdings, and given the proceeds away to his four children. They don't object. He owns a trailer park in Arizona to live in when he wants to be away from Nebraska—so he could move, he could live anywhere. He gives away so much his wife objects, and then he gives away his time, he takes up good works, delivering Meals on Wheels. As penance? As a peek into the future, a window onto old age?

"The past is never dead," Faulkner wrote. "It's not even past."

I let the first package of tapes sit while I finish twelve things. I have deadlines; I have obligations. I don't really want to dive into another unpaid project. On top of everything else, I have to stop the war and save the world or at least protect my son. I call him at a college far from New York City and my finger waggings, to tell him to shake hands with the Quaker who runs the antiwar meetings—it can't hurt. I attend a committee meeting of an organization of writers who are supposed to protect free speech in the world. I call Hillary Clinton's office and surely it's her answering, surely she takes down my name and address with that cool voice of hers and swears that, yes, she will do as I say, thank you so very much for calling. I cook and I cook, three times a day, listening to public radio talk about how fair they are to people who are dismantling the Constitution. I answer the telephone, I remind my son about the Quaker. World War II replays endlessly on one of the TV history channels: footage I have seen so often both as documentary and as fiction that I can't tell them apart. I sit down to write for a few hours and find columns of numbers written in the margins, sums I don't have of the little I make, what little I make, what little I will make if I work on my uncle's story.

When I get around to slitting the box open, what I find first is a note:

Chris is writing this letter for me because my handwriting is not steady. I am sending all the tapes I have so far. It is about 20% of the story. My depression lately has not gotten better so I have not recorded, but I thought I would let you have an initial judgment on the subject matter. The best part of the story is yet to be told as I transfer to the Military Police in Tokyo and Yokohama. Some of the enclosed tapes are copies—not of good quality.

Love, Uncle Don

Four cassettes fall out. Two of them are marked Copies. He has sent me both the original and the copy, probably by mistake. I don't call and tell him. I don't want to insult him by suggesting he's really losing it. I put the copies away and the tapes into my bag. It takes me another week to find the recorder and a day to remember to buy the right-sized batteries.

In the meantime, Dad calls. "There's a little piece of land you should buy with a nice stand of wheat on it."

"You're joking," I say. He knows I don't have any money.

"Ha," he laughs. "Ha, ha. Do you know what the pope said to the bartender?"

I didn't.

"It was something about infallibility," he says. "It reminded me of how people believe things when you put them in books."

"He's finally sent them," I say. "If that's why you called."

"Good." He sounds surprised, as if he weren't always making things happen. "What'd you think?" he asks.

"I haven't listened to them yet. Tomorrow," I say. I don't tell him I've had them for two weeks.

"You ought to get right to it. I don't know how much time he has left."

"What do you mean by that? He's still getting treatment, isn't he?"

"Oh, you know," says Dad.

"Go on," I say. "He's two years younger than you. A veritable baby. What's his secret? Come on."

Dad harrumphs. "Why are you stalling?"

I stare at the wall phone. "I'm afraid I won't be able to do anything with the tapes, I'm afraid they'll be boring and I'll have to let him down, which will be letting you down."

"Stop, stop," he says. "Listen to the tapes."

The hallway the prisoners passed through was where the Japanese had torture chambers. They were oak boxes that looked a lot like phone booths, only shorter. You couldn't sit down in these boxes and you couldn't stand up and after about six hours, you certainly made a point with the prisoners. We marched them past these boxes

three times a day where they could hear these guys moaning and yelling and screaming inside. The other weapon we had for discipline was solitary confinement. It was a hole about twenty feet in the ground with a dirt floor and a sewer lid on top. We'd lower bread and water down about two or three times a day. If you're a guard, getting prisoners quiet is the whole thing, you want the prisoners to stay quiet. [recorded 06/04]

"If you're a guard, getting prisoners quiet is the whole thing."

The Judge Advocate General's rules for the treatment of court-martialed soldiers during World War II were very clear: "Any corporeal punishment, any imprisonment in quarters without daylight, and in general, any form of cruelty is forbidden." This included solitary confinement, breaking rocks, and "sit-down cells," the so-called Japanese boxes.

The longest and funniest—most apt?—title in the military-justice section of the library is *Military Justice Is to Justice as Military Music Is to Music,* written by Robert Sherrill. Although Groucho Marx claims provenance of the title, it is more likely the work of French statesman Georges Clemenceau, who coined it with regard to the Dreyfus case. According to Jonathan Lurie's *Military Justice in America,* "military justice is virtually inseparable from military discipline, which seeks attainment of specific objectives, gained by a military force prepared for death if necessary. Our civilian justice system aims primarily to safeguard the rights of property, community, and the individual."

. . .

"Abu Ghraib is mostly about a lot of generals pointing at captains pointing at anybody else who stands still long enough to be pointed at," I tell my son when he's home one afternoon.

"I thought it was mostly about pictures," says my son. "In demonstrations, students in America got arrested for taking the same poses as the prisoners in the pictures."

"You're right. The trouble was the photographs," I say. "Personnel would have been rotated out and told they were crazy, sick and crazy, for reporting such things, except for the photos."

"Why were they so stupid as to take photos?"

I shrug. "Bad people like to boast just like good people."

"The TV says they were just following orders."

"Yeah, right. They looked like they were enjoying it."

He pulls open the fridge, our point of contact. "The old guys in charge said there was a communication gap between them and the soldiers about what was supposed to be done, what was allowed."

"Maybe the old men were not old enough to know better," I say, watching him pour a glass of milk. "And the contract interrogators. You know, it was too bad they didn't have those disposable cameras in World War Two. They could only watch and remember. I've heard about thirty thousand American troops watching an execution in Italy in 1918 but there was no record."

My son downs the whole glass in one gulp. "Who made the hoods is what I want to know. Was there somebody with a needle and thread or a sewing machine?"

"I thought they just chopped off the ends of supply bags," I say, thinking of the most famous photo. "Chopped off at an angle, so they were peaked."

"Black supply bags?" asks my son.

CHAPTER 10

Years ago, when Chris was perilously close to becoming an old maid, having finished graduate school and already started a practice, she surprised everyone by marrying a short, round-faced Jewish Buddhist lawyer. My uncle's fond of saying that that particular combination ruined all of his best jokes. Her husband practices geriatric law, a good idea in a region of Texas with a large population of retirees. This summer he's spending a lot of time with my uncle. They talk about guilt, Christian and otherwise. Chris and her husband have built a Buddhist prayer temple at the far end of their property, situated over a little stream. This is where my uncle tries to learn meditation from his son-in-law. After a lifetime of making fun of anything slightly left of far right, this act is surely a definitive sign of sheer desperation. My uncle is hardly the meditative type.

All the prisoners had to have all their buttons buttoned and their hair combed. I walked up to this guy and he had one button off his lapel. I took my billy club and tapped that button and told him to shape up before he got to the front of the chow line.

When he reached the front, he still didn't have his button buttoned and I started to say something. He grabbed a serving tray off the stack and tried to slice me in the neck but I stepped inside the door and it missed me. My fellow guard hit the guy upside the head with his club and split his ear, he actually severed his ear from his head. The guy went wild. He started running down the corridor back toward his cell. Myself and the other guy took after him. He backed himself into his own cell, screaming. We locked the door on him and returned to our duties. When lunch was over, I felt sorry for this guy and dished up a tray of food and took it to his cell. It was impossible but he had kicked the wooden ventilator out of the bottom of the steel door and escaped.

I ran outside the cell block and there he was, out in the courtyard we used for drill and exercise. He was just staring at the setting sun, bloody all over. I gently took him by the arm and led him back inside. [recorded 08/04]

I sit in a quiet place and listen to the two tapes to the end, without taking any calls, checking my email, answering the door. All I do is take a few notes.

I call him ten minutes later. I ask whether I can come down and record the rest of the stories myself. I will drop everything and fly to Texas.

"No," he says. I can hear I've embarrassed him. He'd rather record the tapes by himself. He sounds as if he's surprised to hear from me so soon. Even more, he sounds as if I should have called sooner.

"I should have called sooner," I say. "Let me have another tape as quickly as you finish it. I think we have a story here. I really think it might be interesting. Something like—bad boy turns good, the kind of initiation story that people like so much, a *Catcher in the Rye* in occupied Japan."

He laughs but that's all.

I must have missed his point. I say, "I have to make it into some kind of story; it won't go anywhere unless something happens to the main character. You."

"Oh, something happens," he says. "I've lost thirty
pounds so far telling you about it."
"It's the beginning, middle, and end that make a story,"
I tell him. "Life is full of *and and and,* which doesn't
mount up. It's the *but* that counts."
"Don't worry," he says. "It mounts up."
He's not shouting. But this doesn't occur to me until
after I hang up.
Thirty pounds?

At a dinner party in New York, I meet Robert Jay Lifton,
the Harvard psychohistorian who coined the phrase
"post-traumatic stress" for the Vietnam vets in the seven-
ties. "How 'post' is *post*?"
"It's certainly not fixed in time," says Lifton. "Sixty
years? It's been documented."

*About once a month we raided the cell blocks. We went
in about two o'clock in the morning and unlocked all
the doors. One guy reached in and grabbed a leg and
jerked the prisoner out onto the bare concrete floor.
We then searched the cells for weapons. You'd be surprised by the ingenuity of the prisoners. They were sitting in there twenty-four hours a day, thinking of ways
to escape. We found knives, sharp objects shaped from
a piece of rebar from the concrete. We had a lot of sleep-
less nights ourselves. The duty was getting more dangerous.* [recorded 08/04]

CHAPTER 11

Military police grasp the most unmanageable form of power: the brute. There is no city council to inveigh against them. They represent the law as it is understood by the unlawful other, which is everyone else. If they beat up one of their fellow soldiers, he had it coming to him or he needed to be taught a lesson, and that lesson is to obey an MP. The only fear an MP has is the fear of another MP.

Since Kyochan and I were tired of seeking out private places to be with each other, we found a house. Like young kids, we stocked it with food taken from the commissary and from the kitchen in the prison. I had requisitioned a record player from the Bankers' Club. I just walked in and filled it full of records and shut the case on them and walked out like I had a briefcase. We had some Glenn Miller songs and some Frank Sinatra, at that time real modern tunes and very danceable.

MPs from another division and about ten of us got into a little fracas in a small room off the dance floor at the cabaret. This big guy came over and said, "Svoboda, we're going to use your house tonight." I told him no, not in a million years. He pushed me out of the room. We tussled a little but I decided to get my people out of there. I knew we were outnumbered. Somebody jerked the leg off the piano player's stool—the piano player just kept on playing—and started coming after us, him and all the rest of his friends.

The next day I found out that they raided our house and confiscated all the guns and food. They took everything but the record player and the records, which were hidden. When I got over there and saw the place all messed up, I grabbed the record player—it weighed probably fifteen pounds with all the records inside it—and headed back to the prison. You couldn't buy anything like that over there.

I started walking home and got about halfway when these MPs pulled up behind me. I started running. They jumped out of their jeep and started after me because I went up a little alley that they couldn't drive the jeep up. The alley had a curve to it. On one side, there was a series of rock buildings that were solid. On the other side was a bamboo fence filled with Japanese houses made out of rusty metal and anything they could find in the aftermath of the bombings.

I had passed about thirty of them when I heard the MPs catching up because I was still carrying this record player. I looked back—when I was running hard, the curve hid me—but they were gaining on me. I took the record player with both hands and threw it over the fence into this housing area. My god, I must have hit the center pole because it folded right up, the whole house collapsed and the dust flew. Just imagine when the Japanese found out a record player was the culprit— they're getting bombed with everything else, then they get a record player flying in that totally demolishes their home. [recorded 08/04]

I begin a list:

What did Kyochan do for money? Did you support her?

Did she have any family besides her brother?

Did the army try to teach you Japanese?

How did you feel about obeying orders as an MP?

If the stockade was only for American GIs, why did it take in the Filipino kid?

One day we got a fourteen-year-old kid from the Philippines. He had stowed away on an American ship to Japan, solely motivated to come over and kill some Japanese. I thought he was just a nice little kid but he killed four or five Japanese in a park one night. [In the prison] he started hanging around a black fellow we called Jism. He was the leader of the roughest element of the Number Six cell block, and another fellow whose name was Green—we had six Greens in that cell block and they were all in there for the death sentence.

When the Filipino's week was up in solitary confinement, we hauled him up, dropped a rope down and pulled him out. He didn't seem to have changed a bit. [recorded 08/04]

The good-daughter psychologist tends the suicidal dad. What else has Chris studied all those years for, if not for this? But without a job to go to every day, she has no way to escape. Without kids, she can't make an excuse, Johnny has a piano lesson or Mary needs a trip to the orthodontist. Like her other siblings. They do call a few times a week; she does appreciate that. Her older brother jokes with her about needing a sex change in order to take her place, her second brother buys a car wash so he has something to occupy his time when he's not compulsively farming, and her sister tells her she's shopping for Dad—it's a spiritual thing, she says, now that Dad's given out all his money; shopping is what she does best.

What does Chris do best? It's not like her father will lie down on a couch and tell her, or anybody else, for that matter, his problems. He doesn't respond to the pills he does take; he won't try shock therapy again.

Crying is what a lot of women do best, and certainly the situation calls for it. A good cry would relieve her anger, her frustration with him. But he might see it as weakness—or worse, sadness. Or that she's quitting on him, giving up. She's not a quitter.

And she's not a crier. She's statuesque—dark-haired, all beautiful angles of Czech, Scotch, Irish—angles that she doesn't soften. She's more like her father than his son is. "Hey, you," she says to her dad. "Let's get moving."

Lieutenant Michael Drayton, a U.S. National Guard officer who commanded a military police company in Abu Ghraib, said that at the time of the abuse, there was an "overwhelming" inflow of prisoners, creating a chaotic atmosphere in the prison. The 250 military police guarding the prisoners were working up to eighteen-hour shifts.

Our captain seemed to think we could do everything, and kept adding chores. Some of the posts took a half an hour to forty-five minutes to get there and back, if you were lucky. He put us eight hours on, and eight hours off—an impossible situation. [recorded 09/04]

I listen to his tapes several more times. His voice sounds much lower than I remember, it's so gravelly you could walk on it.

CHAPTER 12

*I acquired a dog. A man brought him over from the Philippine Islands. The dog turned out to be a great friend. He came with a name (*Panpan *[meaning prostitute]) that was a four-letter word in Japanese. Every time I called him outside the prison, there were a lot of heads turning. He always went with me through the chow line. I took two trays and always got enough for my dog too. One night after I went through the line, I put the tray down and the dog started gulping down the food. One of the Japanese working there was an ex-officer of the Japanese army. He could speak good English and had the bearing of an arrogant person. "It's too bad the dog gets food like that when there's thousands of Japanese people outside this wall that are starving to death," he said.*

"Well, he didn't bomb Pearl Harbor," I said back.

But that didn't stop the conversation. When he found out I was active in judo, he challenged me to a match. I thought this was going to be just a kind of get-acquainted venture. [recorded 09/04]

I own two dogs that pull me around the block at regular intervals. They especially like to drag me toward the parking lot between two buildings on the Lower East Side where they hear the rooster. Often it will strut out, oblivious to the dogs, its head of red and brown feathers shaking with a cry that echoes weirdly against the tall apartment buildings. It's followed by a couple of fat hens and a Chinese construction worker eating his lunch from a Styrofoam container. He smiles, the dogs sniff closer, the rooster has second thoughts.

I mention the rooster to my uncle during my next phone call. I am trying to pull my uncle into my world, to widen the conversation so we can talk like two people who know each other, rather than like the biographer with her subject, or, more aptly, a niece with her newly discovered uncle. I think New York's rural touch will appeal to him, or that maybe this is the kind of surreal experience that Japan gave him, an unexpected cultural moment on everyday patrol. But his reply is patronizing. He doesn't understand my offer, or maybe he thinks I am changing the subject to myself, my life, when all he wants is to talk about his.

"You can do whatever you want with my tapes," he says. "I think they've got real promise. You can change the story all around, just as long as it's the same."

"I understand," I say. "Do you mind if I send you a list of questions about this and that, details that maybe will lead you to more memories? You'd have time to think them over rather than answer them right away on the phone."

"It's seven-eighths finished," he says. "But go ahead, send me whatever you want."

The exactitude of his storytelling unnerves me. I wouldn't know how long a story was until it was written down and then rewritten at least twice. I start to tell him that I'll need a weight and scales pretty soon when he begins with the pleasantries, all the good-byes. The phone's hung up for a few minutes before I realize what

I haven't heard: no booming voice, no sexy chuckle, no laugh.

The military gives out the most super of superpowers—the right to kill. In exchange, the soldier must forget what happened while he had that right. Since the sixth century B.C., post-traumatic stress disorder has been called variously soldier's heart, shell shock, combat fatigue, battle shock, DaCosta's syndrome, the effort syndrome, exhausted heart, operational fatigue, post-Vietnam syndrome, railroad heart, trench neurosis, and war neurosis. Odysseus wandered the Mediterranean for twenty years, manifesting a different PTSD symptom at each stop—forgetfulness, bullying, depression, hypervigilance, sudden anger—fighting until all his soldiers/veterans were dead.

Dad went through basic training three times. After his first six weeks of training, he asked to go into pre-med. They put him in intelligence. But those people were spies, he says, they died first. He did basic training again and then asked to transfer to cooking school—and went back for a third basic training. He could answer any question during the lectures even if he was completely asleep. Once while he was snoring, everyone quietly moved away so he was left all alone in the middle of the room. The general stopped his lecture and asked him a question. He blinked, stood up, and answered him correctly.

"That's what kept me in shape," says Dad. "Conservation of energy."

The judo gym was in a city park about a mile away. We [my uncle and the Japanese cook] drove over to the park. It was probably nine o'clock and pitch-dark. We climbed over the fence. Inside were a swimming pool and a gym with rice mats. We put on our judo outfits and he grabbed hold of my collar, in the typical judo move. I got his but I felt right away he was a hell of a lot stronger than I thought he was, and a lot more agile. We threw each other a couple of times and got up and all of a sudden he became very aggressive and flipped me down to the ground and tried to choke me. Fortunately, I was younger and stronger, and I got him in a bad kind of arm hold. This wasn't judo at all, it was just survival. I damned near broke his arm, then hit him in the head a couple of times. I got in the jeep and left him and didn't regret it at all. This guy was out to kill me. I drove back to the prison minus one Japanese. He never came back to the prison. [recorded 09/04]

What it feels like to be occupied. To have lost.

I receive another set of tapes from my uncle, but I don't call him. I'm beginning to feel as if it's an obligation, this back-and-forth, or that I'm patronizing him by saying how good they are. Besides, I don't want to hear he's worse—he can't sign his credit-card slips, he can't push his chair back from the breakfast table; that wouldn't be fair, I'm just getting to know him. And if he gets worse, so will my Dad, I reason with my own theory of relativity. After a thorough investigation of my dread, three days pass and I dial him up, but no one's home.

I mail him more questions. I hardly know enough to form them, but I try to make them leading.

Tell me how the other MPs felt about the Japanese.

What did your father think of you enlisting?
What was the most frightening thing that happened over there?
What's your opinion of Abu Ghraib and the MPs?
Did you tell Dad everything that went on?

Questions circling the question: what's your secret? the one I can't ask because I'm not supposed to know anything about it. Like most people these days confronted by a personal letter, he ignores it. Also letters require a presentation of self more tangible than words evaporating into air over the telephone or microphone, and perhaps he doesn't want that self any more real.
Dictation as consolation.

"He said he was going to have to start executing the prisoners, the ones in the death cells."

Captain Miller, the one with the big stomach, called a meeting for all the MPs in a large room in the auditorium. There was only one company of us so we weren't that many people. He commended us for being good soldiers and doing our job well and having a minimum of problems. Then he dropped a bomb. He said the prison was getting overcrowded, terribly overcrowded. He said he was going to have to start executing the prisoners, the ones in the death cells. [recorded 09/04]

INTERLUDE

Cabaret music. Two soldiers at attention, one an MP in a full-dress uniform, white helmet, white gloves, white armband, facing the other who's wearing an apron over khakis. Both tote toy guns.

MP
I could be in Nebraska. All the rice for wheat, all the crows for cows.

COOK
Dad cried when I left.

MP looks over his shoulder, positions his gun, faces front.

MP
This could screw up my life.

COOK
I'm outta here, I'm gone, I'm home. I'm not allowed to say.

MP
These Japs could be packing big lead. I have to walk around all the time talking sweet. Cootchee-coo.

COOK
(doing a little dance)
Occupy my body, occupy my soul. You've got to keep rice in that Jap bowl.

>MP
>It's an economic miracle.

>COOK
>Take up judo and throw them on their backs.

MP takes off his white gloves, inspects them.

>MP
>A few girls would be good.

A loud noise. The two of them fall to their bellies and stare out into the darkness.

>COOK
>That was the stock market.

>MP
>I'm bleeding already.

MP waves his gun around.

>COOK
>You were writing a little letter to the girl next door?

MP rolls over and pulls a piece of paper from his pocket.

>MP
>It's about two words long:
>Dear Girlfriend . . .

>COOK
>Say love, love, love.
>Don't tell her anything.

>MP
>Nothing, sweet nothings.

MP finds a pen and writes feverishly.

Sound of honky-tonk, light/dark/light of klieg lights from a nightclub. The two of them jump up. The light plays over them.

MP

What color are you?

COOK

I'm your brother.

MP takes a step closer.

MP

What color is that?

COOK

I've always been your brother and you've always tried to shoot me.

MP

I can't shoot you.

They throw down their guns and embrace. It turns into wrestling.

MP

Can you keep a secret?

COOK

You obviously aren't going to.

The MP flips him to the ground.

MP

I don't trust anybody but you.

COOK

You could dance to that.

COOK jitterbugs in the air, cockroach-style.

MP stops him and leans toward him. The COOK shakes him off.

COOK

I love you too.

MP

No, really. You have to keep this a secret for sixty years.

COOK

No.

MP

Yes.

MP whispers in his ear.

COOK

You did?

MP

You don't believe me?

The MP takes a swing at him. They wrestle furiously. The light dims until it's pitch-black.

A gun goes off.

II

The next four or five weeks were hell. He found a group of Japanese carpenters and they hauled in enough lumber to build a big house. They were working and banging and hammering right smack between the two death-cell blocks. That's where he was having the gallows built. I guess he wanted to hold down on expenses. It was a stupid thing to do because the prisoners became extremely nervous and dangerous.

It took about two and a half weeks to build and a day or two to test it. They tripped the platform—it was just a three by three piece of wood that the guy stood on, with a beam going across the top—and then they dropped the trapdoor out from underneath him. The prisoner fell the ten feet and that was it.

That was the theory.

He ended up draping the damn thing in black silk, which I thought was in bad taste. [recorded 09/04]

Lieutenant Black is the stockade commander in Jack Pearl's *Stockade*, a novel published in 1965 about abuses in military prisons. A pistol-whipping, sunglasses-wearing, riding-crop-carrying caricature of Evil, the commander provides a very accurate explanation of the military's attitude toward its prisoner-soldiers:

> Let me point out that the prisoners in this stockade, in their own peculiar way, have undermined the military potential of the nation as effectively

as any enemy. They have not only disqualified themselves from service, but they have also deprived the Army of the services of the men who must detain and guard them—you and I.

"Don't you have buddies from that time that you keep up with?" I ask my uncle.

"No," he says. "The unit disappeared."

"A whole unit?" I say. "Go on."

"I've mailed you another tape," he says. "Tell me what you think."

I write to the National Personnel Records Center for my uncle's official military papers and discover they burned in the great National Archives fire of 1973, along with thousands of other servicemen's records. The MP Museum hasn't heard of the 483rd MPEG, nor has the Military Museum, nor has the National Archives. Even Google is stumped.

My uncle's had it with the medical people. He insists on leaving Texas and flying back to Nebraska. He wants to go home.

The first time in my uncle's life when he wasn't in control occurred when he had to "carry out orders," wearing those white MP gloves. The second time in his life is now over.

At the airport, he kisses his daughter good-bye on the lips, a sorrowful thing it is so unusual.

About ten years ago, one of my uncle's neighbor's bulls kept wandering into his cornstalks, my dad tells me. That isn't so bad, giving your neighbor a little free feed, but when his bull, a real Romeo, makes his way through the fence over to where the cows are clumping together next to the water tank, that's different, you get a little upset.

Dad says his brother calls up his neighbor and asks politely if that bull can be pulled off his heifers pronto. A week later, his brother goes around to that section to see which ones are pregnant and finds the bull is into them again. He and his son use their pickups and three-wheelers to encourage the bull to move out of the field. It trots off without much trouble so he decides that is the end of it and fixes the fence even better than before. Next thing, he is out there aborting one of the heifers, actually working on one of them done by the bull, when along comes that bull again, charging right through the fence and jumping on them again. He gets so mad he hops into his pickup, drives home, collects a rifle, drives back, and kills the bull who is still at it; he kills the sonofabitch with a single bullet to the head. He has the renderer out there so fast the neighbor doesn't know the bull is dead until he gets the bill in the mail a week later.

"Are you sure he wasn't storying you?" I ask.

"I was there for part of that," says Dad. "I helped fix the fence."

I am driving Dad past that stretch of fence now, the fence that also caused Dad's heart attack. He fell asleep and drove into it and hit his head on the steering wheel so hard he suffered a blood clot.

He yawns now. "That family can tell stories, and that's the truth of it. Say, I've got a title for his book. You can call it *My Brother Don*."

"Good," I say. "That means you're going to write it."

Dad gives me the eye. He says to turn at the next corner, he's going to show me something.

Officially, there were no escapes.

I am coming home from an all-day session in Tokyo and the prison siren goes off. I am about fifty yards from the

gate when I turn around and start walking away. It is
dinnertime and Captain Miller has on a big white nap-
kin wrapped around his immense stomach. He catches
me and yells, "Svoboda, come on back." I have to turn
around and retrieve my gun. We kept our automatic ma-
chine guns and shotguns in the gatehouse. We take a
jeep because it is a great distance around the prison. We
think the prisoners are trying to get out via the storm
sewer, a big drainage tube that runs underneath the wall
and out into a ditch. When we pull up in front of the
spillway, we hear voices in the back of the tube and can
tell there are four or five prisoners in there. The captain
says, "Jism and you, Number Six, and the Filipino—if
you're not out of there in two minutes we're going to tear-
gas you." He waits about thirty seconds and turns the
tear gas on. We think they'll come running out. There is
all this yelling and screaming and we don't know what
the hell is going until here comes this big wad of barbed
wire out of the end of the sewer. Just like one of those ice
cream cone push-ups, but it comes out real slow. They
don't hardly have a stitch of clothes on because they are
all so torn up with barbed wire. [recorded 09/04]

People were not expected to express any emotion in the
1950s. The returning vets of the Greatest Generation
kept quiet about the horror they witnessed, they inter-
nalized it. Any negative reaction to all the death they witnessed would sully the sacrifices of the dead. Some of
this survivors' guilt was ameliorated by the applause and
ticker tape showered on the vets when they returned.
That celebration said, *Good job, you're the hero, every-*
thing you did was worth it.

Toward the end of the war, the army drafted anybody:
sentenced criminals, sixteen-year-old kids, mental defi-

cients. It was planning a mass infantry assault and just wanted bodies. Later, during the occupation, it was especially grateful to get the draft-age boys. Battle innocent, they were less likely to hold a grudge against the people whose country they occupied. But they witnessed the damage the war had done and they were the ones who had to try to repair it. Part of that damage was the battle-worn GIs who had gotten into trouble, as well as the hastily drafted misfits who ended up as prisoners in the stockade. Unfortunately, the young MPs didn't get any applause when they returned.

But why should any of the vets complain about post-traumatic stress when so many of them got rich quick in the 1950s? Besides, if they did complain, the psychiatric hospitals never let anyone out. Later in the decade, the new drugs tested in those hospitals allowed the patients to leave, but just then about the only treatment that sent a patient home was a lobotomy.

Dad drives over to the feedlot. It's not a big operation; it's just a place where the cattle get fed while they're waiting to get picked up by the commercial feeders. A barn, a lot of fence, troughs and water pumps. "Do you see any sick ones?" he asks me. He has to separate out the sick ones.

I say that one is drooling, and he says that happens. "How about the limper?"

"Maybe," I say, and he says, "We'll see," and says he'll drive now. I step out of the high cab into the muddy other world of cattle and dung, walk around the front of the truck through the milling herd that watches me so closely with their big brown eyes, I feel as if they might eat me instead of vice versa. I'm glad to see the inside of the truck again. I'm about to say so and why, when he guns the truck straight at the sick cow.

It bolts. Chasing it, we bounce hard into and out of gopher holes and run straight up a big dunghill. I'm terrified that Dad's head will hit the roof of the cab and another clot will start its way up to his brain, but he's not afraid, he's in hot pursuit. The cow shoots off into the far corner of the field.

Dad does a 180 and drives after her, drives her into a corner and then eases her along the fence. There's not much distance left before we reach the feedlot gate when she bolts again, runs right in front of us, and escapes back into the herd. Just then two more pickups come riding over the gopher holes, my brother's and his hired hand's. Dad must've said something in code to them when he walkie-talkied his afternoon's instructions earlier. Even when I'm driving, he's in control.

All three vehicles converge on the sick cow's end of the herd and then that cow is done for, that cow gets herself backed into the lot. Dad squints at her while she trots to the far fence. "I don't know," he says. "You could be right. We'll give her antibiotics there and see how she does."

"I thought it was off to the rendering plant."

Dad curbs a sorrowful look. "A nice-sized cow like that? Another six months, and it could be worth a thousand dollars. We'll let it hang around and eat cornstalks for a while. But here's one that does have to go."

You can see its chest heave.

"I gave it shots a couple of weeks ago," Dad says. "I think it had some kind of bad flu."

"Mad cow?" I say.

"Those are Canadian cows," he says, not dropping a beat. "But did you know your aunt died of mad cow, and the woman your mother's brother married after that? It was the meat in Hawaii."

He says *Hawaii-ya,* the way they do. Hawaiian meat, foreign enough.

"I don't know," I say to him. "It sounds to me like he just had a really deep freezer."

Dad laughs. "Let's go to lunch and eat hamburgers." He waves to my brother and his helper, who stay to nudge the chest-heaver into the pen with the other.

"But what does chasing sick cows around have to do with your brother?" I ask after we turn onto the main road.

"He ought to be back in the world with the rest of us, depressed or not. I'm going to see if I can't sell him that land he sold me back to him, at a profit. That ought to bring him around."

When we get home, I check for messages of my own on his machine. Halfway through a week's worth of hang-ups and ranch talk, I hear his brother's voice, twice, asking him to *please pick up, why don't you pick up, I'm your little brother and I'm sick.*

I am shocked. Is Dad so heartless?

"Yeah, I heard that one. I talked to him," says Dad. "It's an old message."

Shock treatment is the preferred therapy of vets because it is considered punishment, a VA nurse tells me.

"No problem if they start the draft, Mom. I will go to Canada and take an entrance test there and get into their law school."

"You can do that?" I ask. "Remember, I lived in Canada during the Vietnam era and it wasn't so easy even then."

"I saw how to do it on the web."

"What site?"

"The Canadian site, what do you think? And if I don't want to take the test for law school, I can just go to graduate school there."

"You're sure about that? And what about your girl-friend?"

"She can go too. It's easier for a girl."

Deflecting the conversation with my own experience is so parental. "What about work there?" I say instead. "You have to have money to live on and papers to get a job."

"Oh, I'll work. Don't you worry about that."

"Me, worry?" I say. I don't tell him I worked under an assumed name and social-insurance number for a year, terrified every moment that I would be deported. What I do say is, "What was the address of the site?"

"I don't know. I don't remember. It's not important."

Each prisoner had a transcript of his trial and he'd sit around all day, talking about the trial and mulling over what could have been and what couldn't. [recorded 09/04]

Dad tells me on the phone that a priest absolved my uncle, telling him it was all right for him to abandon his preg-

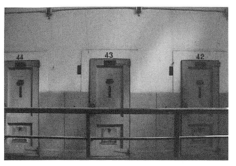

"Each prisoner had a transcript of his trial."

nant Japanese girlfriend, even if they did have a Shinto ceremony to make them man and wife. There was no official way of bringing her home anyway, and he didn't want to stay in Japan.

"A country remembers the occupation better that way," he says, "with lots of little slant-eyed Americans running around."

"I did read that MacArthur had the chaplains discourage the soldiers from thinking they were really married."

Dad clears his throat. "He knew it was a boy. She must have had it while he was there."

"Or she wrote a letter in that English he taught her."

Led by one leanish woman showing lots of midriff, twenty-six of us get into position. We heft our weights to take out the turkey wings. Right arm, left. But with us it's more than vanity. Lifting weights builds bone that otherwise will break and land us in the hospital in twenty years, with complications often fatal. We lift so we won't break, so we won't die.

My uncle, aged eighteen, lifted weights to come alive. Muscle building was what kids did then, in the middle

of America, in the middle of Japan, in order to become someone. Then a whole life of one-two, one-two, one-two-three, the habit of exercise. For my uncle, a yearling hefted over his head, a son lifted high on each arm. *Put me down!* Always getting stronger and stronger until—
Surely one of his sons knows when his strength, its arc, steadies and slides. Sons test.
I have to remember to breathe.
I breathe but I don't think. I pump and then the clock says to stop. Exercise is supposed to be escape, but for me, it's the opposite, total immersion. There's a task to be completed, it's good for you—that's plenty of motivation for me. But there's always a point where I have to think—no, it's not thinking that I do, but forcing the will—when I have to lift or push too much and I have to invoke some brain in my arm to do it, I have to think with my arm.

My muscle shows when I curl a bicep. That's what my uncle has, control of his body skin-level, muscle-deep. Control is a very seductive goal. I remember turning forty and noticing a thickening in my upper arm, my waist, my brain, and being surprised—I'd done nothing different. Now I have to exercise to ward off that thickness, to keep at least the bones strong. I watch the others lift their weights in unison in the mirrors. We could be all one mind as well as body, all of us in a trance, wondering about my uncle's urge toward the superhuman.

If I could only keep up with the leader.

At my uncle's height, he looks powerful already; even now he doesn't have to ripple or pop buttons or clutch at his fingers to flex the top muscles of his arms.

Like Dad, he wears glasses. Unlike Dad, he wears black frames over his baby face, Clark Kent–style (once more on the left). Superman. Like Dad, he probably can't see a thing without them, is quickly reduced to baby sight and squalling (once more on the right). The only time men remove their glasses is when they're making love—or fighting. They just get in there and hunch their backs and go after whatever blob presents itself.

My uncle was the first Caucasian in the world to earn a black belt.

As a child I thought having a black belt meant something was really great about your clothing.

I stagger home, my right calf pulsing from whatever I've done too much of.

As the days rolled by, the idea that we are really going to execute the prisoners starts to sink in. [recorded 09/04]

"As the days rolled by, the idea that we are really going to execute the prisoners starts to sink in."

Abu Abu Abu—we get the point, we don't want to hear about it anymore. Change the station. Media burnout.

Just what those culpable count on.

This is not the simplistic sixties. I understand better now that there's a complicated economic machine that runs our country, which saps our emotional and political strength rather than energizes it. I also understand that we are in Iraq to "liberate" the people. I do remember, however, what "liberate" meant in the sixties. Is there some technical difference in meaning? Defense

Secretary Rumsfeld has said, "What has been charged thus far is abuse, which I believe technically is different from torture. . . . I'm not going to address the 'torture' word."

Someone at the top okays torturing Iraqis, ignoring the Geneva Conventions.

Someone at the top okays executing GIs in Japan. No convention for the GIs.

Bring in the guilty bastard is the British adage for a military trial. The American is even more telling: *Give the man a fair trial, then hang the son of a bitch.*

It takes an average of fourteen minutes to die in a hanging American-style, with a cowboy noose. The British use a hangman's knot and their condemned die instantly of a broken neck. The American's noose causes slow strangulation—or sometimes the head is jerked right off the body, which is what happened to Saddam Hussein's half brother when we hanged him.

Prior to hanging, Americans require the ritual of a final meal, then standing for six minutes while the charges are read, after which the condemned is always asked if he has anything to say. These days, however, the condemned doesn't even get the last word. The prison's PR department edits his speech, according to Robert Jay Lifton and Greg Mitchell's book *Who Owns Death? Capital Punishment, the American Conscience, and the End of Executions.* Then it's—*Get on with the job.*

One indication of the army's "guilty before proven innocent" philosophy was, according to the House of Representatives' Committee on Military Affairs report, that "an accused enlisted man's pay stops, not from the day of his conviction, but from the day of his arrest." Although there are no figures available for the occupation, in 1940 aquittals in general courts-martial averaged a mere 4 percent.

The Dirty Dozen, starring Lee Marvin and Donald Sutherland and many other famous actors, opens with a GI being executed for something he denies he's done even as the hood is pulled over his head. MPs stand stony-faced beside him while the sentence is carried out; the MPs wear helmets that look just like a World War I doughboy's, only white, and they also wear white armbands and white gloves. I'd forgotten about the white helmets and the armbands—but not the gloves, the handwashing, no-fingerprints-left-behind white gloves. *Don't make me get my hands dirty* is what they suggest. The MPs wore them in Japan too, the country where white is a sign of death rather than innocence.

If the movie was really "based on a true story" as the publicity boasts, it should have shown nine black soldiers condemned to death to conform to the statistics. But only one black man stands for them all, although someone named Jimenez plays the guitar and gets shot first in the prisoners' insane raid on a German stronghold.

Nineteen forty-six was the year a black veteran had his eyes gouged out with a billy club in Aiken, South Carolina. It was also a time of lynchings, of racially motivated executions that people kept quiet about for decades. In 1946 Paul Robeson spoke in Madison Square Garden in protest of the lynching of four people in Georgia: a black serviceman who had just returned from nine months in the Pacific, his girl, her friend, and a man accused of pulling a knife on a white man. Twelve to fifteen unmasked white men lynched them in broad daylight, shooting hundreds of bullets into the two couples. But no one was indicted, no one arrested, no one charged or punished, and the FBI didn't reveal what they learned in their investigation until 1992, when someone finally came forward to testify.

It was also in 1946 that Lieutenant General Robert L. Eichelberger wrote to the 8th Army stockade: "It is desired that an additional report be submitted . . . to be titled or marked 'White,' which will include offenses committed by all military personnel not of negro ancestry."

Every Sunday we had different services, Methodist, Presbyterian, or Catholic services in the auditorium. We would go into the cell blocks and blow the whistle and say, "Anybody for Methodist services?" and all the shingles would pop out, every one of them. We'd unlock all the doors and march them into the auditorium and then they'd have the services. Boy, were they solemn. Then we'd march them back and say, "Anybody for Catholic services?" and all the same shingles would come popping out, and everybody would go to Communion and we'd march them back to their cells. One day a rabbi showed up. Of course all the shingles came a-popping out. They all got seated and just about filled the auditorium. The rabbi walks out from behind the curtain and looked up and saw all those black guys and I thought he was going to run off the rear end of the stage. [recorded 09/04]

It gets cold in that part of Texas. Chris can see her breath some mornings. She can't always be holding it.

CHAPTER 15

Years ago my uncle bought a ranch-style house two doors from the cemetery. Then he sold it and bought the house right next to it. He was always looking for a bargain. The neighbors say that before he got sick, you could see him walking around the tombstones every afternoon after his golf game. The sidewalk peters out long before his house, so that is the only walk he could have taken to get away from the traffic, such as it is in their small town.

The cemetery is a good place to think, is what he tells everyone.

By the time he gets home, he has lost a total of forty pounds. "Atkins thin," he calls it. "Good for the cattle business." His wife puts whipping cream in his milk shakes and butter in his burgers. He tells everyone it's not her cooking, it's the roads in Texas. "Why, you could starve to death between restaurants," he says. "The roads are that long. Sometimes when you get out of the car after one of those drives, your legs have forgotten how to walk and you need food just to touch the ground."

I hear he tries to make his homecoming easy for everybody. He watches a lot of football with his grandkids. "Hand me the phone," he says to his son, "and I'll place a bet on the bowl game."

We were riding in one of those troops-carrying type of trucks where they have a bunch of men on either side. There were about twelve of us in there, picked up from different stations. Everybody was tired and grouchy with

*our eight hours on, eight hours off regime. I was the last
one off the truck. I was in a hurry and took my clip out of
my carbine and shucked out the shell. I didn't notice
whether the shell actually fell because when I pulled the
trigger, I shot right down the hallway. It was a miracle I
didn't kill anybody.* [recorded 9/04]

My parents are not your average farmer and farmer's
wife. Both have advanced degrees. Although rabid Re-
publicans—my father was a delegate to every convention from Goldwater on—they couldn't send my epileptic
brother to Vietnam. My uncle's elder son also didn't
serve. Did he have epilepsy too, or was it a matter of
class? Gentleman farmers, like characters in an Austen
novel, avoid conscription. Or is it that my uncle is smart
and sensitive and didn't want his son to endure what
he had endured, even postwar? In the Midwest so many
veterans of World War II insisted their sons serve.

I wish my uncle would call me back.

A white boy from Jersey named Hicswa killed two
Japanese in Tokyo two weeks after peace was declared.
He had just spent eighteen months trying to kill every
Japanese in sight. He was sentenced to hang but the
public was outraged, even the Japanese government
suggested lenience. A fifty-five-year-old man from the
United States wrote in to the *Stars and Stripes* and offered to be executed in his place. "He has his whole life
in front of him," wrote the man. "It wasn't his fault, and
I'm pretty much washed up." The court received 53,536
letters from the public, including 106 letters from the
House of Representatives, 79 letters from U.S. senators,
48,708 signatures on 288 petitions, 5 letters from Spanish

War Veterans posts, 8 from Disabled American Veterans posts, 108 from VFW posts, 94 from American Legion posts, 46 from War Mothers organizations, 21 from Polish organizations, 45 from labor organizations, and many, many more letters protesting his sentence.

In contrast, sometimes black soldiers condemned to death were not allowed to speak up for their defense during their courts-martial. A *Time* magazine article announcing Hicswa's pardon rationalized Truman's decision by saying that "Pentagon lawyers could find no precedent of a U.S. serviceman's having been executed for the murder or rape of a German or Japanese." A week later, it published a letter to the editor from a soldier with the 2nd Armored division who recalled "a number of special orders posted describing the death sentence having been carried out for rape-murder."

Hicswa spent time in my uncle's prison, and escaped. The *Stars and Stripes* reported that he was quickly found in a local brothel. After an MP threatened to break down the door, he came out willingly, pulling his pants up.

A capture too good to be true.

According to Dad, an officer asked my uncle to take the rap for Hicswa's escape. He said my uncle plead guilty to neglect of duty and got off, just as the officer promised. Why did my uncle agree to take the fall? Had he done something himself? I add these questions to my list. But I don't call him, I don't want him to know that Dad's feeding me stories too. I'm hoping he'll tell me about it on the next tape.

You'd take out about a dozen, march them out the front gate and almost around the prison to where there was an area of tangled-up trees that they were cleaning with axes. Oh, no, they wouldn't have had axes—do you know, I don't know how in the hell they were doing it, they were breaking up these branches and piling them up so they could be hauled off. Anyway, one day I had Number Six out and they were having a bit of a break

and he got up and walked over to me and said, "I'm going to go over to this whorehouse and you're not going to do a damn thing about it." I didn't say anything, I just tucked the shotgun up right underneath his throat and pulled it off safety.

That was the closest I ever came to killing somebody. [recorded 09/04]

"Guards . . . stared out the same bars."

Guards often feel trapped with their prisoners. Perhaps this was especially true in the Eighth Army stockade, where the guards were using the cells as their quarters and stared out the same bars. Hicswa's mother complained about the conditions under which her son was incarcerated. She forced an inspection that confirmed only that both guards and prisoners suffered.

We started taking the prisoners out of their cells, and letting them run free outside the wall so we could sleep in their beds. [recorded 09/04]

Someone tells me about my uncle waking in an inmate's bed and seeing the shadow of a hanged man dangling over him. I say "someone" because I ask my father and my sister and husband and son—and no one remembers whose story it was. Could my uncle have told me? I don't remember ever getting so personal with him. But the image is so precise—my uncle opens his eyes, and because he's not wearing his glasses, the shadow over him is indistinct but so clearly dead. When he wakes up, it's to a nightmare.

I can't call him and ask him about this either, it's too morbid, he's already too depressed.

I'm proud to be my uncle's confidante but frightened. Why doesn't he tell all of this to someone trained to listen, someone who can figure out whether this is what's bothering him? But if I urge him to talk to someone else, I won't get the story.

I don't really listen though. I don't listen enough. I am just the one he's talking to, I am the witness. His wife can't be the witness, as she is implicated, she is the one who waited at home for him to return, she's part of the story, the woman he left his Japanese son and wife for. He has to return to her and not talk. He can't talk to his daughter. She is his daughter. When I finally get him on the phone again, he's cheerful, he's happy I called, he's just finishing the last tape—that's 95 percent of it, he says, and soon he'll mail the rest off. He'll get to my questions later.

I postpone calling him again until I get the last tape, then I can't call him until I listen to it. I can't listen to it. I'm too busy. I have to make a living. I don't have time for all these war stories. Please.

The captain accomplishes what he sets out to do and that is to get more room in his prison. [recorded 09/04]

He isn't home but a couple of days. He won't go to church with them that Saturday night, it doesn't do him any good is what he tells them, waving them off. Then he isn't home when they return from Mass. No one can find him anywhere.

Dad has a hunch. Look in the long barn where he keeps his pickup. Dad warns them not to look themselves but to wait for the sheriff.

They don't wait for the sheriff.

CHAPTER 16

I wave my son away; I take the phone waving—a little privacy—but my son watches me, sensing calamity, and I wave at him again, listening, then I wave at the phone as if it's something hot I shouldn't touch, then I sob.

I didn't call him is something I can't say out loud or it will be truer than it already is. I should have called him back just one more time to tell him how great I thought his stories were, and, *Send me some more.* Or just, *Hi, thanks for still being alive, I know it hurts*—that kind of call.

I didn't call.

Silence everywhere on the phone and from me and my softhearted son, home for the weekend, watching me cry.

"He's not your dad," says my son.

For a few minutes, I can't talk. I say something on the phone and hang up.

"Look at the size of your shoes," I say to my son. "You're standing in his feet."

He puts down the recruiting folder he's looked at all three colors of and takes me by the shoulders. "They're my feet."

I cry all over again, fearing for him, grieving for my uncle's end, saddened by the secrets men share.

"Here's a good picture of him, all muscle. He's holding a calf, three hundred pounds at least. That's the kind of

picture they liked to take in those days—we have one of
your father too." It's the night before the funeral.

My uncle had no patience because he was so quick. He
could see through the situation and know the solution
and not want to hang around for it to work out. Other
people call it a low threshold for boredom. When you're
young, such a proclivity gets you into trouble. Like when
he was at the recruiting table and punched the officer
in the jaw for making a crack about his bohunk plaid
jacket because he knew he couldn't hit an officer once
he was in. That kind of thinking ahead.

When you're old, the trouble could be terminal; you
could see what was coming—death—and do it yourself.
That's what his kids think. His daughter says it had nothing to do with his tour of duty. Dad says they're a secre-
tive bunch, and he knows his brother better about this
than they do. His daughter says he made one more tape,
but when she produces it, there's nothing on it. Curiously,
on the back side there's a bit of a news report accidentally
recorded in the middle, a radio report on Abu Ghraib.
She doesn't know how it got there. "Nobody was in the
house but us," she says. "No one could have broken in
and recorded it. It must've been caused by an accident,
by Dad erasing something."

There it is, in radio-recorded whispers: *Abu Ghraib*.

I still don't listen to the last tape he sent, not right away
and not in the week after the funeral. I can't. Before he
died I was just too busy with all my excuses, each of
them about me and not him, or about him smothering
and silencing me with all his stories—I have other stories I have to write—and now his voice is the last thing

I want to hear, that voice so full of charm and wit and intelligence, husky and tired and low, sad and sweet. I should have reached him. I should have called and called. As a writer I know what it's like, having a story, needing someone to say, *Go on, it's great, it's worth the pain, the trouble.* But now I have to know if he told me the secret, I don't have the rest of his life to coax it out of him.

I find a soft chair and put on a good pair of headphones and smile at all the places where he wanted me to, and stare into the wall. His recorded voice now sounds full of suppressions, hesitations, and dampened enthusiasm.

The death sentence prisoners are very hard to handle after that. They make hostile moves for you and threats, and it is just a miserable environment. [recorded 09/04]

So that's where the tape ends, the gallows built with its drapery of bunting, the two wings of condemned men forced to look at it every hour of the day. Or maybe it ends elsewhere and his daughter or son erased the rest of it. Or maybe he meant to go on, to set the record straight, to tell about how he was exhausted from those eight-hours-on, eight-hours-off shifts, and he fell into the bed of one of the executed, still warm, and slept and woke to the sound of someone's body—someone he knew—dropping, and the shadow of the still-swinging rope. They were always executed at one a.m.

Two Zen monks come to a river where a girl is weeping on the bank. "Please help me," she begs, looking out at the swollen waters. "I have to meet my family on the other side." Although his order forbids him to touch a woman, the first monk lifts the girl onto his shoulders and carries her across the river. The two monks walk on in silence. After a mile or so, the second monk can no longer restrain himself. "Do you realize you've broken the rules of our order?"

"Are you still carrying her?" the first monk says. "I put her down on the other side."

Guilt, it's hard to get rid of.

The funeral is so small-town the undertaker reads the name off the card of each bouquet before the service, and about half those bouquets were purchased at Safeway. We are soon parked in its lot again. Somebody has to get milk for coffee. The shotgun's sitting upright between us just in case Dad spots a pheasant—or a terrorist. If it's loaded, from where it sits it will shoot off Dad's nose and my ear.

We're both so quiet, the word *dumb* seems right. Words don't cover meaning very well after a funeral, but eventually we say them anyway, slowly at first, scrambling for anything.

I tell him I read that 940 people committed suicide in 1935 by throwing themselves into a volcano. "They thought their vapor would go straight to heaven," I say.

"Maybe it did. You've seen heaven, haven't you? Lots of vapor." Dad is looking out the side window into the nearly empty parking lot.

Dad says his brother spent his last day with his son. They drove all the way to his son's new farm in Rushville, talking about land and football. "They had a great time. He even made a bet on Sunday's game."

"He was so weak he couldn't roll up the window, was what I heard."

"That's just what they said. I don't know," says Dad. "Why didn't he get electric windows for that truck?"

"I heard he misspelled something in his note, which is highly unlike him."

"Not that we know what the note said." Dad sighs and shakes his head. "Maybe it was a murder. Maybe he wrote it at gunpoint."

"Dad."

"Anything is possible."

"That's the problem. Your mind doesn't want to light on the one thing that is ninety-nine percent likely, that he would actually take the coward's way out."

"You have to be brave to stare down the barrel of a gun, any way you look at it," he says.

"You close your eyes," I say.

"I failed to save him," says Dad. "It's about being the brother. I saved his ass plenty of times when he thought he could box his way out of the world."

"Did you ever fight with him?"

"We didn't fight like other people fight—we wrestled. We wrestled a lot. Sometimes I won. But when he did judo on me, I was a goner."

The Safeway doors slide open, slide closed.

"What was it he didn't want anyone to know? Maybe he told me in the tapes but I couldn't tell what it was."

Dad clears his throat. "Well, I guess he's dead now, and I can tell you. A man doesn't have to go to his grave with someone else's secret."

A late tumbleweed snags on a shopping cart.

"He killed someone," Dad says. "That was the secret. He told me just as soon as he came home from the service. He got all agitated after that and convinced me to take the train to California and bum around for a while. That glass in his arm that bothered him so much he went to Mayo—that must have reminded him all the time that he'd killed somebody."

"He says he didn't kill anybody on the tapes."

Dad shakes his head slowly. "All I know is that I couldn't tell anyone about it for all these years, and now I'm telling you. After all this time," he says. "Some prisoner he made friends with in the chow line, they got into a tussle and the gun went off."

"But—"

Dad says he only knows what his brother told him.

Two men, wrestling.

"Thank you, thank you," says his daughter at the wake. "You kept him alive all summer."

"Me?" I say. "You kept house and home for him, took care of your mother, quit your job."

"It was the tapes. He loved making them, he lived for your calls."

"Thanks," I say. "Thanks." I can't eat my *kolache*, I can't talk to anyone else.

III

"Executing GIs?" says my husband, reading one of my early drafts. "That doesn't sound right. Especially not in Japan. That would be terrible for morale."

It's the summer after my uncle's depression, eight months after his death. I keep moving through the oppressive part of his narrative blindly, focusing on scenes of his high jinks, like when he tried to teach the Japanese girls in their tight kimonos to jitterbug. I don't want to think about my charming uncle being involved in anything so dreadful as executions.

I tidy my notes, which means that I abandon myself to speculation. Did the captain think that because the condemned prisoners were black, nobody would notice if some of them were executed? Were things that chaotic? Maybe he executed a prisoner who wasn't condemned because nobody would be following his case that closely. Would the man just be declared missing or escaped?

According to the *National Law Journal* in 1999, the United States has executed only 135 American soldiers since 1916. According to the 1946 report from the House Committee on Military Affairs, the military executed 141 in World War II alone, and the report mentions that "the full statistics of military justice during the war period have not been compiled due, it is said, to shortage of personnel." In 2000, the Statistical Abstract of the United States shows 160 men executed between 1942 and 1962. A list of 154 executed men was discovered shoved behind a desk in 2003 during a cleanup at the Pentagon. They were executed between 1942 and 1961, according to Richard Dieter, head of the Death Penalty Information Center. How many of them are on the committee's list of 141 is unknown—there is no access to that list. Many on the Pentagon list are noted with just a last name, some without a date of execution, none with a location.

I have to talk to somebody who was there. I call my uncle's rivals, the 720th Battalion, who trashed his love nest with Kyochan. I speak to their officer in charge of reunions. Has he heard about executions at the Eighth Army stockade? The man gasps. He says they would never execute soldiers there, like that, then. I ask if he might put me in contact with one of the vets who shared the stockade with my uncle. Eventually he gives me the name of a vet, but he remembers nothing. I email Professor Robert Lilly, a criminologist famous for a study of the executions of eighteen black servicemen in England during World War II. His report shows 169 executed between 1942 and 1961. "There are several 'unsolved' or unconfirmed execution stories like your uncle's," he writes. "Send me all the details you find." But he doesn't give me any leads.

Dad says, "Sure, they were executed in Japan. It cost plenty to ship them back and put them in prison at home. It was efficient."

"Hitler was efficient," I say.

Dad laughs. "That's inflammatory. If I know the army, you'll have to find the bodies."

I hear the ex-judge in his voice.

Who tells any war story is what is important; that is, who has the authority to tell it, and then when and why. Point of view is also important, but the military uses a heavy hand when it comes to point of view, their history, that story. What for the military constitutes a true story? The voice of a general? Documents signed by authorities? Dead bodies in neat rows? Not the testimony of its soldiers. When questioned by the military establishment, veterans' accounts have always been disallowed—the anecdotal evidence regarding Agent Orange, the Gulf War Syndrome, the effects of depleted uranium on military personnel; contested statements about who really ordered the slaughter of Korean civilians at No Gun Ri—all ignored for decades.

It is only with the advent of tiny cheap recording devices that the common soldier has any power.

All suicides produce questions about the story of a life. The questions with this one proliferate with all I don't know about his tapes. I thought I was following a tidy coming-of-age account of a young soldier in postwar Japan. Instead there is this mystery of possible executions, with the site of those executions seven thousand miles away.

CHAPTER 18

Tokyo is sweltering. That word conjures up sweat in rivulets, not these open-air cafés cordoned by jets of air-conditioning. What climate crisis? My husband and I pass dozens of these cafés on our bus trip to Nakano, one of the least glitzy Tokyo neighborhoods. How did activists ever get the Kyoto treaty off the ground in Japan? But despite our fears about global warming, we certainly regret leaving the bus's air-conditioning for the city's hundred-degree heat and humidity.

Fordham, where I have a two-year contract as the writer-in-residence, has awarded me a research grant. I am in Tokyo to search for the Japanese elderly who might have worked in the stockade's kitchen, or as children might have played around its walls. Maybe I can find records of incidents, escapes, or executions lodged somewhere in bureaucratic Tokyo from that most chaotic of times, the postwar period. At the very least, someone might have written about the prison or at least taken a few pictures.

Nakano prefecture was home to the Eighth Army stockade until 1953. Once fifteen or so miles from Tokyo and now swallowed whole, Nakano's fame today rests on its anime and *manga* markets, where shop after shop of books and toys is stacked horizontally and vertically in a mall just outside the train station in an area known as Broadway, where black markets stood in my uncle's time. Left of Broadway is the location of Nakano's other dark industry, an elite World War II spy-training center, later headquarters for the secret police but now torn down.

About a ten-minute walk away stands what's left of the stockade's last wall and its brick entranceway. The rest of its ten acres have been razed and replaced by a baseball diamond, a running track, a library specializing in Japanese prisons, a school for prison guards,

"Nakano's fame today rests on its anime and *manga* markets."

and a gift store of objects made by prisoners. All of this is positioned over a huge underground water-processing plant.

But we do not yet take the tour. Ron Sherman, a sixty-seven-year-old Texan expat dressed in a smoke-stained Philippine four-pocketed shirt, with a scraggly gray ponytail down his back and a cigarette always in process, meets us at the Broadway markets. He is an internet acquaintance of one of the stockade guards I've contacted and, like many of his generation who didn't go to war, he's fascinated by it and has volunteered to help me. It's only later we discover he's right of Genghis Khan, but perhaps this should have been obvious in light of his interest in all things military.

Today, in this awful heat, he's bleary, often wiping his eyes behind his blue-tinted John Lennon sunglasses. We walk first to his place, giving us a chance to soak up Nakano's atmosphere; the twisting streets with sidewalks lined with potted plants and the occasional pre-war structure. Because I've never been to Japan, every detail pointed out by Sherman distracts me from the heat. "Here is where the prostitutes hung out, here is where the car pool was," says Sherman, gesturing toward various apartment buildings, offices, and intersections. "And here's a building from the old days," he tells me. It's his, all three stories abandoned except for his self-proclaimed first-floor "hovel," two rooms of wall-to-wall chaos. Several fans move the heat away from a nest of ancient computers but do nothing for the cigarette smoke wreathing the tiny sweltering space. When I mention that the summer my uncle served was the warmest recorded in twenty years, Sherman's face twists into a perfect replica of a Japanese warrior's grimace. "You ain't seen nothing yet."

After a thorough explanation of his thriving eBay business reselling Japanese sake cups that he scrounges from castaways, he downloads aerial photos of the stockade he's collected onto our memory stick, and we plan our investigation. Hours later, after many digressions, including how he trained a wild boar to hunt pheasants in Hawaii, we drink "red beer," a concoction of hot sauce and ketchup stirred into a quart of cheap brew designed to obliterate the heat in an alcoholic buzz. We agree to meet at the public library the next day with the translator, his friend Hikaru. Even after thirty years of living in Japan, Sherman speaks only pidgin Japanese.

Idogoya Cho Japan
January 29, 1946

Dear Character of Characters,
Tis time I should be catching up with my
correspondence. No! To put the situation bluntly
and brief, I, Pfc Svoboda have been shirking

my duty, but as a true M.P. my motto is (a jerk
that shirks is a shirking jerk) "ex sompthin." To
make the picture a little more clear, I should be
wandering aimlessly through Yokohama park,
poking my arm band into every bodies business
but I am not that kind, as you know I like to be
alone in parks with certain people too "ruff ruff."
(wolf noise, I think).

It's only after I return from Tokyo that I receive my uncle's
service letters from my aunt. In her grief, she couldn't
part with them any sooner. Two years is very little time to
recover from a sudden death. I'm grateful.

To me the misspelling of "every bodies" suggests that
he's already met Kyochan in the park. It's about the right
time, according to the date of the letter. You can practically hear his wolf whistle. Does my aunt know the possible subtext? Or is his premarital self so young that he's
another man entirely to her?

Sherman says Kyochan can't be traced. Many women
are called Kyo, and the *chan* is just a diminutive.

In summer, in winter, Dad played tennis with his brother
on Saturday afternoons and on Sundays after church.
They played on the court beside the town pool because
no one ever put away the net. Although my cousins lived
only a half hour's drive away, these games were the only
time we saw one another. It was our job to sweep the
court. Once ash covered it from a nearby brush fire, once
two feet of snow drifted over half of it. We worked as a
team, sweeping furiously to have it ready for the game.
While they played, we competed to retrieve the balls or—
very rarely—flipped a coin to see who'd get to pop the
vacuum seal of a new can of balls.

We must have cheered too, each for his own father, our side with six cheering, his with three. I don't remember one father winning more than the other. I remember afterward the two fathers with drinks in their hands, standing up in the kitchen waist high with kids, my uncle always in a hurry to leave but always telling jokes as fast as he could make them, and everyone showing off, from dance steps to height.

What's an uncle's suicide? Since I didn't know him well, it's not a major personal tragedy. My early drafts show me calculating the delivery of his story for its greatest shock value—*Poor me! The niece who thinks she killed her uncle through inattention.* I was trying to make his death all about me, which is, to a greater or lesser extent, what the living always do to give death meaning. Death drags us too close to meaninglessness. But I certainly don't suffer the daily reminders of the living that his immediate family do.

What about the woman who has to carry on, Superman's wife?

Dad and I visit her on one of my trips home. She's still beautiful, charming, offers us wine in the middle of the afternoon, and talks about a trip to Russia she's looking forward to. Composure is what she radiates. *Do not feel sorry for me.* Is this dignity or anger? Why not both?

Our *ryokan*—a tatami-matted, futon-laden hotel room— is situated in Ikebukuro, an area that redefines the concept of a bedroom community since every block features love hotels renting rooms by the hour. "Even married couples use love hotels, particularly if they share small quarters with in-laws," our Frommer's assures us. It also mentions a recent trend in which twelve-year-old schoolgirls trade sex for Gucci bags. Billboards depicting prepubescent—or barely pubescent—girls sprawled so their transparent blouses fall open set the neighborhood's mood, as do the huge crows circling them. Having once spent six months on a Polynesian island where sex was the currency, not money, I begin to rethink the notion of sex pan-Pacific, especially postwar, when twenty-year-old American boys met Japanese women whose men had no jobs and whose children were starving. Not to mention 1.9 million widows.

The country already had the geisha.

"The true geishas before the war never engaged in prostitution," according to the *Soldiers Guide to Japan.*

March 3

*Tis cherry blossom time and all the geisha gals
are turning in their winter hair and teeth to
cope with the coming season, but as yet B.T.O.
Svobodio has not yet been stung by the butterfly.*

*Here is knocking you a kiss,
Love from the Yokohama Yokel*

His letters—so endearing, intimate and guilt-ridden. By now, my uncle would have furnished his little hideaway with Kyochan.

Three librarians at the Nakano public library offer all the books and illustrations on the prison they hold, which are few. A picture of the devastation in Nakano after the firebombing is particularly arresting: a blackened vista, all charred ruin. Placed next to a shot of the cells that the guards slept in, with the gallows and the condemned prisoners just a few steps away, the bleakness might be complete for a homesick guard.

No, says my husband, not quite. He says every time anyone poked at the ruins, the stench rising from it must have been terrible. He's a 9/11 veteran and knows first-hand what it feels like to be attacked, the out-of-control fear, the smoke, the rubble—the smell.

Hikaru Kasahara, our translator, tells us that the prison first held Japanese political prisoners. After the Americans left in 1953, it was returned to the Japanese to house dissident writers. Hikaru works as the managing editor of a journal critical of the Japanese government. She is fascinated and terrified by any material we uncover. When the head librarian discovers a video about the prison, their final offering, Hikaru readily checks it out for us, she's anxious to see it too.

Packing up, I offer the three helpful librarians little gifts, but they refuse. "I thought gift giving was traditional."

"They are government workers," Hikaru explains. "Exempt from gifts."

We all smile, especially Sherman, who tells us that in 1989 he unearthed human remains while fooling around with his metal detector in a vacant lot in Shinjuku, an area a few train stops away. They turned out to be those of prisoners of war tortured in the Japanese Unit 731 experiments. "Vivisectionists—those experimenters were government workers too," he says, with a wicked grin. He'll tell me more about Unit 731 later.

We canvass the Correctional Library of Japan, which is located right next to the remains of the stockade wall. It contains no written material we haven't already seen. I tell Hikaru I'm surprised that all those incarcerated dissident writers didn't write about the prison. "Maybe they did," she says, "but I don't think the work would be published now or then."

The librarian surprises us by producing twenty new photos. She can't conceal her pleasure at seeing our enthusiasm, although none of the pictures show the gallows or the torture boxes my uncle spoke about, or even people. Sherman mentions that they used to have an exhibit showing leg irons. Would leg irons lead to torture boxes? Hikaru can't get any clear information about where the artifacts have gone.

Outside, we tour the prison wall, now half its original height, with the platforms and lookouts removed, and stop at the beautiful Bauhaus brick entry that was preserved from the wrecking ball. Beyond the entry lies a series of fishponds built by the Americans, which Sherman says will be surrounded by fishermen tomorrow. "People who rebuild from ashes don't move," he says. "I'll bet some of them remember what was going on in the stockade."

We pass a cemetery next to a shrine, and Sherman notes that the Japanese take another name when they die, "so their deeds don't follow them into the afterlife."

"They must shy away from biography," I say.

Unit 731, Sherman tells me, was the Asian Auschwitz, biological experimental-warfare stations that murdered up to two hundred thousand POWs during World War II. Hundreds of units existed in China, Manchuria, and Japan. He hands me the research. The documents refer to victims of 731 as "logs." These logs were in fact live subjects, mostly Chinese soldiers and civilians but also captured Russians, Brits, and Americans. For thirteen years, the POWs were frozen alive to research frostbite, burned alive to research human combustion, loaded into vacuum chambers until their bellies ruptured, hung by their ankles to see how long a person could live upside down, infected with plague, anthrax, and cholera, and subjected to vivisection without anesthesia.

"It's because the prisoners thought that we were doctors," said Dr. Toshio Tono in the *Baltimore Sun*, May 28, 1995, about the eight captured American flyers who were brought into a 731 unit in Fukuoka. "Since they could see the white smocks . . . they didn't struggle. They never dreamed they would be dissected." Another physician recalled "joining other doctors to watch while a prisoner was shot in the stomach to give Japanese surgeons practice at extracting bullets. While the victim was still alive, the doctors also practiced amputations. . . . They wanted to learn whether a patient could survive the partial loss of his liver or if epilepsy could be controlled by removing part of the brain."

The bones Sherman unearthed in 1989 were found during the construction of the new National Institutes of Health (NIH), the site of the old Imperial Army Medical College, and also the location of the "Epidemic Prevention Laboratory," which employed many ex–731 scientists. Examination of these highly contaminated bones revealed that they were the skulls and the thighbones of 101 people, according to Professor Keiichi Tsuneishi of Kanagawa University, an expert on Unit 731. Many bore bullet holes and sawtooth marks. Only one was Caucasian. "The seven hundred thirty-one doctors just tossed out the bodies with the garbage when they were done with them," says Sherman. In September 2006 an eighty-four-year-old nurse told the *Japan Times*: "We were going to be in trouble . . . if American soldiers asked us about the specimens."

The United States allowed the 731 scientists to go

unprosecuted in exchange for their data. Many former members of Unit 731 became part of the Japanese medical establishment. Dr. Masaji Kitano, major general in charge of Unit 731, led Japan's largest pharmaceutical company, the Green Cross, which manufactured blood products that were found, in the mid-1980s, to have been infected with HIV.

"The moral of the story is," according to Sherman, "bury your bones deep."

Where would an executed GI lie buried in Japan? There is no Plot E, the cemetery in France where the military buried all who were executed in the European theater. Officials at the American Battle Monuments Commission, the Joint POW/MIA Accounting Command, Graves Registration and Mortuary Affairs, and the Army Casualty and Memorial Affairs Operation Center tell me that under no circumstances were any bodies of our military left in Japan.

But now we have bodies showing up, at least Unit 731's POWs. Although a guard writes to me to say that the body of the GI he remembered executed in the stockade in 1949 was given over to the man's wife, those executed earlier might have been temporarily buried or even casually buried. We never find anyone to ask if bones were uncovered during the building of the waterworks, or why there is an area undeveloped within the park, in the middle of Tokyo, surrounded by some of the most expensive real estate in the world.

While my husband and Sherman prepare their red beers back at the hovel, Hikaru and I look into the records at City Hall. Banks of computers punctuate messy workstations as far as the eye can see. One city worker refers us to another, phone calls are made, questions restated, printouts consulted. For detailed information they frown and suggest we contact the Law Department, or even the Ministry of Defense, about postwar crime statistics—*but what about the archives in your own country?*

Hikaru turns to me. I've already begun that search.

Leaving City Hall, we are immediately lost. "Where are we?" has been Sherman's mantra at every street corner, surely one all foreigners mutter in Tokyo, with its unmarked or renamed or unnumbered intersections. In this heat and traffic, even Hikaru wishes we had Sherman to guide us back. This morning we had used my husband's GPS device whenever Sherman became disoriented. Now we're without it, and we wander through the streets while Hikaru asks our way, shop by shop.

The big blank of unfathomable Tokyo reinforces in me the unlikelihood of the Japanese having kept track of our GIs in the chaos of their own mortality in those early postwar months, when, in April 1946 alone, some 267 bodies were found in the streets of Tokyo.

We finally arrive at Sherman's while an elderly man is securing his bicycle across the way. Inspired by all the information Hikaru found at the library, she asks him if he's old enough to remember the GIs, the prison, the postwar frenzy of rebuilding. "Of course," he says; he's eighty-seven. Even Hikaru is surprised—he's very fit. He laughs and tells her right here is where his aunt housed someone who worked in the prison and brought food back as rent. He himself was stationed on an island off Tokyo and watched the city burn.

They exchange no more than five sentences, but both he and Hikaru are now near tears. She has never heard stories about the war before from anyone. Her father, a professor of English literature at a Japanese university, died young from cancer, and her mother committed suicide. "No one talks about the war personally," she says.

"It's all about the antibase movement now, getting the U.S. to stop their continued occupation of Japan, especially in Okinawa." She invites us to join her and her Canadian boyfriend in Shinjuku for dinner. I begin talking about the film *Lost in Translation* three blocks out of Shinjuku Station. Hikaru is impressed— this is where one of its more memorable sequences was filmed. More Times Square than Times Square, even and especially the electronically hyped-up version of the last five years—and twice as populated—the area obliterates any sense of time except the future. We eat at a Thai restaurant on some floor in the middle of an office building and meet Monty DiPiero, her boyfriend, an art critic for the *Japan Times*. He's also worked in commercials and movies as a token Caucasian—and impersonated a priest for marriage ceremonies. "People want some kind of ceremony," Monty says. "And the pay was good." His friend Julian uses his costume now.

"That was probably how your uncle got married," says Sherman. "Whoever he had shacked up with probably paid someone to wear a Buddhist robe and make it look official."

"No," I say. "He was a Catholic. His mother sent him a missal in Japan."

"Your uncle was depressed about the abortion Kyochan had to have," he insists. "In Japan, aborted babies grow up and haunt their parents in their old age. There's a shrine for these babies right next to where the stockade stood."

"He told his son he had a Japanese baby," I say. "He wouldn't have done that if she had aborted it."

"We'll go visit the shrine and ask the priests if they have any records," says Sherman.

But Hikaru has to work tomorrow; she has a magazine to publish.

CHAPTER 19

My husband and I take an air-conditioned train to a bucolic Japanese version of Knott's Berry Farm, a village of ancient farmhouses relocated to Kawasaki City. Although each beautifully spare dwelling exudes the usual Japanese museum-quality minimalism, I suspect clutter in real life, the historical moment messy with gear and pots and clothes drying. A different charcoal—eucalyptus, sage, scents I can't place—burns at each farmhouse. We rest at a steep-roofed chalet where they serve fans with the cold noodles, the watermelon, and the smoky iced green tea. We fan and look over a faux mountain path, meditating on executions.

"Why would they go to such expense to build the gallows if they weren't going to use it? I mean, they just finished the war, they should've been celebrating."

My husband says, "Deterrence. They wanted the soldiers to fear the place. The threat of not knowing when it would be used was their weapon."

"Maybe it was just a threat." This idea relieves me.

"No, to be effective it had to be used on someone. You have to find out why, and why MacArthur would risk bad publicity on an execution he could have arranged back home."

When we return to Tokyo, we watch the prison video, with Hikaru translating the voice-over. The son of its architect narrates, showing off the main building's striking brick façade with great pride before the bulldozers and wrecking balls attack it in 1980. The camera-man finds its empty interiors dark and moody. The wooden doors of the cells look hand hewn, antique, as attractive as those of farmhouses we toured. In one shot, I think I see the outside gallows, at least a set of isolated steps that leads to a plat-form. Further on in the film, there are shots of the cells designed in an X, where the MPs slept at its center. The cameraman cannot resist shooting the butterflies fluttering outside the bars.

"... designed in an X, where the MPs slept at its center."

The Japanese architect modeled the stockade after the Eastern State Penitentiary, a design that has been dupli-cated by at least three hundred prisons worldwide. Planned in part by Ben Franklin and built in 1829 by Philadelphia Quakers, the prison was supposed to create "penitents," that is, inmates were to reform by meditating on their crimes in silence. All the cells face outside rather than toward each other. Guards even wore slippers so they wouldn't break the solitude, and the prison's X de-sign allowed them to easily hear inmates who did. In the case of the Eighth Army stockade, that meant that death-cell prisoners looked only at the gallows.

We've arrived at the end of the rainy season, "which is at the beginning of the typhoon season," Sherman says, laughing. Today we are armed with umbrellas, but it's only our sweat that drips. We make our first stop at the fishing pool where, as Sherman had promised, fisher-men are screwing their aluminum benches in place and snapping together ten-foot-long poles and pole holders and all manner of other gadgetry for luring the big carp swirling uninterestedly in the three-foot-deep water. No one catches anything, nothing even nibbles. Perhaps this is why they don't mind talking to Hikaru. She squats next to them while I hold the umbrella to shield us from the intense sun. The fisherman on her left says that the first words of English he learned were "Give me chocolate." A second fisherman, sweating, draws a complicated figure in the dirt. I first think it is a Japanese character, two boxes, one inside the other. Hikaru explains that it is the perimeter of the stockade surrounded by the houses of prostitution. The fisherman tells Hikaru that most of the women involved were thirty years old and from elsewhere. "This war happened because people in high status wanted it and these women were earning foreign currency, therefore they were contributing to Japan. They were considered useful," she translates.

I tell Hikaru that several books I'd read suggested that the prostitutes were the true cause of Japan's recovery, not the coal-mining or textile industries. She laughs.

Hikaru is a very beautiful thirty. She wears her hair pinned flat to her head, emphasizing her large and intelligent-looking eyes. Perhaps this is the real reason the fishermen don't hesitate to speak with her. But she is all business, careful to drain all the lasciviousness out of our questions, using, for example, *sex industry* for *prostitution*. Walking to the other side of the pond, Sherman points out that Hikaru and I look like two missionaries, both of us dressed in black, under a black umbrella and carrying open notebooks.

A third fisherman, rolling bread crumbs into balls for bait, remembers only a few details about the period after the war. "The destruction was shocking," he says. "Just surviving it left that time a blur." The last fisherman sports a pencil mustache and won't look at either Hikaru or me. Speaking with a sharp bitterness, he remembers trading a priceless antique Japanese sword for a can of GI oatmeal.

His response delights me. I'm elated to have found someone who contradicts the usual grateful, docile, and happy portrait of the defeated Japanese. His anger gives me hope that I might have a chance to find out what was really going on in the prison.

I want to talk to someone who actually worked there, who might have seen the gallows, who might have had something to do with my uncle sixty years ago. Sherman agrees that my goal is not as far-fetched as it sounds: he repeats that anyone who lived nearby who escaped the scorched devastation would have a close connection with the area and probably would not have moved.

"For example," he says, "the Shinto shrine has stood in the same place for the last four hundred years." He explains it was saved from the firebombing by a bucket brigade of the faithful. On one corner of the grounds stands the temple dedicated to aborted babies. "For obvious reasons, geishas often set up near these temples," says Sherman. While we dip out water from its holy well, a middle-aged woman washes the little red-caped statues representing the babies and leaves an offering. "A very lucrative situation for the monks," says Sherman, "in light of the number of GIs in the vicinity back then."

". . . the little red-caped statues."

While Sherman and my husband reconnoiter the grounds for shade, an acolyte whisks Hikaru and me inside the main site's air-conditioned quarters. Amid lace-covered furniture and cups of cold smoky tea, the priest in charge lectures us on Japanese-American history. The San Francisco Treaty, in 1952, was the end of U.S. dominance, he tells us, not the declaration of peace signed at the end of World War II. Hikaru doesn't go into the occupation of Okinawa. He insists that no military had married at his shrine before 1955, the year he took over the records, and certainly this would be where they would marry, given the shrine's size and importance. Hikaru whispers to me that perhaps Sherman's theory of a bogus wedding is right.

Although the priest began to work at the shrine too late for my concerns, he wants to validate his position as a leader in the community. Hikaru nods as he goes on and on about what he remembers of the GIs in the 1950s. I have lots of patience for their exchange since we are so air-conditioned, but finally I get to the point: I tell him I believe that my uncle committed suicide because he was haunted by something that happened in the prison.

The priest brings tears to my eyes by saying he admires my quest, that in Shinto beliefs, it is important to put the spirit to rest, whether mine or my uncle's. I haven't considered my spirit, the one that is pushing all these people in this heat to discover what happened to my uncle's ghost, or just the ghost of his ghost.

My husband and Sherman have collapsed under the shade of the roof over the holy well. We stagger several blocks to an air-conditioned supermarket, where the two of them take a very long time selecting cold snacks. Hikaru and I decide it's a great place to waylay exiting old women with our questions. We station ourselves just outside the air-conditioned doors. The first woman we talk to moved to the area too late to answer anything. The second, a hunchbacked eighty-eight-year-old with a perfectly round face straight from Japanese iconography—even Hikaru says so—has nothing detailed to tell us. While a mist of cold air rises off her crippled figure, she bottlenecks the exit with her heavy bags. We must move on.

At the Nakano Historical Museum, the curators can't find any books we haven't already seen at the other libraries, but Sherman and my husband meet a T-shirt-clad worker who turns out to be a country-music aficionado— "I like country music too much"—who also chased the soldiers around the stockade for chocolate. "The daughter of my mother's friend, a Buddhist, was involved in the sex industry there, but she is now dead," he tells us. Born in 1946, he says that he and his childhood friends assumed executions occurred in the stockade every time smoke rose from its chimneys—cremations!—and that sirens were common, signaling escapes. Although the prisoners were usually found in the surrounding brothels, these escapes frightened the locals because they involved desperate men. He was also afraid of the black soldiers who trained as boxers. He says the GIs looked down on the Nakano people because the soldiers were tall and the Japanese were small and very weak—from hunger and from lack of weapons. Even the Americans' uniforms were more "cool" than theirs. But most of the Americans were quite kind and that was why he married a Japanese-American woman. He even named his daughter Lisa, after Presley's, and sings us the same bars of Elvis that his prime minister had serenaded Bush with the week before. Ghost stories? After the prison was torn down and the area covered over with a baseball field, he noticed that five or six players had broken their legs on second base—right where the gallows stood.

We nod. Now we know where the gallows stood, at least where they were rebuilt a few years after my uncle left, in consideration for the inmates.

We are halfway down the street when my husband and Sherman exclaim: "Born in 1946? It's your uncle's son!" They insist we go back and ask him about his father. The idea is so far-fetched we have to dispute it. Hikaru devises a couple of questions to conceal our real interest. He's happy to keep on talking—but his father, he tells us, was too old to serve in the army and died in 1950. He waves us off. His thick black hair, his handsome profile, his flirtatious ways—it is easy to see him as my uncle's son.

We decamp to the site of the prison itself. Now known as Heiwanomori Park, the far end of the grounds features a cluster of cement picnic tables under cement slats of shade, and a sluggish creek. The first two old men we meet are smoking and reading newspapers and tell us they are from elsewhere, but the third, putting out scraps to feed the multitude of feral cats, talks eagerly even though he has a speech impediment. He tells us that prostitutes used to give him chocolate. "One girl was in charge of forty of them and they used to follow the patrolling pairs of MPs while they marched around the raised platform of the stockade," he says. Some of these women rented rooms for the Americans and themselves. They told him to keep away from the Americans because they would kill him. One of the guards threw tobacco down from the platform. Sometimes others threw over the skins of potatoes. They were peeled so poorly he collected and cooked them. Once he heard a woman screaming nearby, but he knew he shouldn't get close, and he was afraid of the black soldiers anyway.

May 18, 46

*The only excitement comes when there is a
prison break, which happens about 2 times a
week. We each take about 6 clips of ammo and
raid the geisha houses, after we shoot out all the
street lights and break the doors down and find
everything from Russians to merchant marines
and not the prisoners, we usually go back and
find them in the chow line half starved to death,
cause they can't eat fish heads and rice.*

Yours faithfully,
Don

The afternoon has turned officially typhoon—hot and
windless and more humid—but still two old men walk
quickly around the running path that covers another
area of the reclaimed stockade grounds. One of them
wears purple glasses, the other wipes at the unending
sweat that escapes his sweatband. They are so excited
answering Hikaru's questions they interrupt each other.
They tell us armed American soldiers made their prisoners cut the grass outside the stockade. They remember
hearing gunshots at night and assumed those were from
escapes, but the wall was really too high to know what
was going on inside. They did notice when the United
States brought in three hundred sex-industry workers for
what the men called "a festival." The children of these
prostitutes were sent to an orphanage in the Kanagawa
Prefecture or aborted. When the stockade was given back
to the Japanese, these prostitutes moved to Tachikawa
Air Force Base.

We now have a pretty good picture of how the relationships between Japanese women and the MPs worked—at

least from the Japanese male's point of view. When we spot two older women under shade umbrellas at the park's edge, we pounce on them. Both women put hankies close to their mouths while they talk—a sign of heat prostration or the intimate nature of their revelations? Before the U.S. Army came, they tell us, the stockade was dark. Afterward, it was brighter and made them feel more secure. But the escapes frightened them because they assumed the men would hide under their houses (that's where they hide in Kurosawa movies). Otherwise, the only time they saw the prisoners was when they cut the grass, which they did very sloppily, compared with the Japanese prisoners years later. When they were finished, an MP would come out with a big bucket full of milk for them to drink, which made one of the women quite angry because even the prisoners were fed better than the Japanese. They saw few black prisoners. They thought that was because the blacks had the more serious offenses and didn't get to work outside the stockade. Everyone, even the prisoners, was quite young—and so tall and handsome. They tell us that Japanese women tried to get close to the soldiers to get chocolate and favors. They themselves never dated any, even though they were twenty and twenty-one at the time.

We bow and thank them. "Surely they are lying," I say to Hikaru. "The prostitutes must've had some competition." Hikaru smiles but doesn't answer. We spot several black Japanese children. Of course they could be the legitimate offspring of a contemporary union, but still I want to ask them whether their grandmothers were prostitutes. Maybe, within the tradition of the geisha and all the modern manifestations, this is not such a non sequitur in Japan, at least not to an adult. But how would we meet the grandmothers except by receiving an invitation to come to their homes?

Hikaru tells me no Japanese would invite us in. "At least I think not," she says. She has been astounded by the candidness of the replies so far.

Again and again the Japanese exclaim over the size of the American GIs. Supermen, that's what they were. As if to confirm their opinion, the GIs brought the Superman comic-book hero with them. He first appeared in the United States in 1938, when most of the soldiers were around ten, an age ripe for identification and fantasy. What the soldiers left behind was the seed of anime, that business that now flourishes so vibrantly in Nakano.

My uncle, Clark Kent, the bespectacled man with a secret.

Our last interview for the day is with an eighty-eight-year-old woman who is watering the racks of potted plants that flank her house. She remembers the club a few blocks away where the servicemen danced in

"How lonely she is!"

1946, then she leans on her wall and moans. How lonely she is! Her husband fought in three wars, and just behind her, behind the flowers, is where she dug her bomb shelter while he was away. For twenty minutes she gestures and cries about her loneliness, until Hikaru has to tell her we have other old people waiting to tell their stories. I say to Hikaru I'm surprised we haven't encountered more overwhelming loneliness, given the isolation that old age usually brings. Nearly every time we conclude an interview, we are told that there is no one else to talk to, that everyone else is dead. But then we meet the next old person, sometimes standing only ten feet away.

Hikaru apologizes for not getting more specific answers about the executions. "We can only do that if we find someone who really worked in the stockade," I tell her. "But you're getting me details to surround the subject, the only way I can make the past real."

My husband and I drink only cold tea and go to bed early.

Maybe dreams will lead us on.

CHAPTER 20

World War II vets are dying at the rate of 1,500 a day. I'm a little luckier in that the occupation is about a minute postwar, and in that the vets I'm looking for are that much younger. But I still fccl the pressure. Before I leave for Tokyo, I want at least oral corroboration of the existence of the gallows. I start tracking down vets via the internet.

At first it's too easy. I contact the Korean War vet A. G. Corey who says, "Sure, I remember seeing the gallows. They were still there in 1952 when I passed through there as a guard."

"Oh, they hung a lot of people in there," says Billy F., a personnel officer for the Eighth Army stockade, in an internet interview conducted by the Eastern Oklahoma Historical Society. However, the historical society is reluctant to allow me to contact him directly; they will only release his wife's email, not his telephone number. His wife says she's undergoing surgery and doesn't have time to write things down. She says Billy doesn't hear very well, so talking to him on the phone won't work. She suggests that I stop by. She is put off when I tell her I live in New York City. I wait until her surgery is over and email her again. She says she's recovering, but the surgery didn't go well and Billy went to the hospital too. "Stop bothering us," she emails. "What is it you want so much?" I compile a list of questions to probe around my one single interest, the gallows. They will get to answering me after the holidays. I email them after the holidays. They still aren't feeling very well and discourage me from emailing again. I am conciliatory; I plan to email them in a few days with just a single question: how many were executed? That way I'll get both a number and confirmation that the executions occurred. When I reach her again, all she'll tell me is that in 1950 her seven-year-old daughter caught polio in the swimming pool that was built for the stockade, and the commanding officer forbade them to warn anyone else. "Isn't that terrible?" she says, but she still won't let me talk to Billy. "It upsets him to talk about that time," she says. "He's at the end of his life. He needs peace."

"We thought we had managed all right, kept the awful things out of our minds, but now I'm an old man and they come out from where I hid them. Every night," a vet tells author Richard Holmes in *Acts of War: The Behavior of Men in Battle*.

I wonder about pressing my new friend Frank S. for details. Frank is another guard I found via a contact on the internet. He says he knows a lot and will tell me about it in his next letter—but not to call him. Susan Delmaestro, a psychiatrist with the Philadelphia VA hospital, tells me that when the news about Abu Ghraib broke, her Vietnam-vet patients confessed they had done so much worse and feared they would be next to take the stand. "The more serious of these wartime parallels have grievous consequences for both victims . . . and perpetrators, who in time reenter the U.S. population as damaged veterans," writes veteran Michael Uhl in "Vietnam's Shadow over Abu Ghraib." Delmaestro suggests that by talking to the vets I'll be pursuing the Heisenberg uncertainty principle of interviewing. That is, just by asking about the trauma, I might cause more trauma, even more suicides. Those who do talk about their war experiences usually tell stories of survival, those who don't often harbor stories of guilt. She says talking to Frank might be quite dangerous if he's never told his story before. I need to know what support he has, who he would go to if he became depressed.

After Frank assures me he's well taken care of, I write him a letter with just enough of my uncle's anecdotes to tease him into telling his own, and I bury my primary question, *How many?* hoping, once again, that a mere number would be the least traumatic for him. In the meantime, I review Greg Hartley and Maryann Karinch's *How to Spot a Liar: Why People Don't Tell the Truth . . . and How You Can Catch Them,* a book more about self-incrimination than prevarication, written by an interrogator who has worked at Guantánamo. My liberal leanings make me feel guilty for even opening the book, but I feel I need it; I have no natural inclination toward subtlety or manipulation. I am the bad detective, the honest peasant; I assume that luck and native intelligence and the goodness of people's hearts—or their underlying desire for revenge—will get me what I want.

Frank's return letter sounds lonely; he says he likes to have people to write to. He encloses a picture of himself leaning against his sheriff's car; he tells me all about the lakes in his region. He writes:

Seeing a man after he was hanged is not a pretty sight . . . I dream of seeing things I wish I hadn't seen . . . As a guard there are things I can't tell you.

An Australian researcher discovered that sixty-two percent of older World War II veterans—men without the diagnosis of post-traumatic stress—had at least monthly nightmares.

I mail three cassettes with self-addressed return envelopes to other vets I find on the internet, figuring that an interrogation this impersonal wouldn't be traumatizing. The cassettes return unrecorded, one with a kind note from the head of the local American Legion, apologizing for the man's death.

. . .

This is my form letter:

I am particularly interested in the safety and welfare of those who served as guards at the Eighth Army stockade because my uncle suggested it was a difficult duty. Inmates were desperate to escape after the gallows were built, which made the work especially hazardous. Anything you might remember about your duty at the time would be helpful in piecing together the history.

Then Nick P. answers my letter. He is delighted to hear from me. He's not really interested in talking about guarding the stockade—they had a great time, hoisting beer up to the guards on the catwalk and riding bicycles around its perimeter—but he wants me to write the story of his stowing away on a Japanese boat after his tour of duty. I wrestle him back to the subject by asking about escapes, and he says he doesn't remember any at all. He was, after all, stationed there three years after my uncle. But wait, he says, there was one guy. Somehow he broke his arm coming down the stairs after we caught him. And after he got out of the hospital, somehow he had two broken arms.

In Philip Zimbardo's famous 1971 Stanford study of prison abuse, college students were arbitrarily assigned the role of jailor or prisoner and were expected to stay together for two weeks. After only six days, the prisoners had become so demoralized and abused that the experiment was ended. "Unless there's strict leadership, unless there's clear leadership that prevents the abuse of power, that power will seep out. That power, that sadistic impulse will dominate," Zimbardo said during a May 11, 2004, PBS interview concerning Abu Ghraib. Robert Jay Lifton said in the same program: "You're more likely to have atrocities in this kind of war . . . and in this case when it turns into an occupation, the atrocity potential is sustained."

My uncle's tapes do not sound confessional; he never sounds as if he was doing anything other than carrying out his duties. I too am carrying out my duty by trying to figure out what happened. But in no way does my review of my uncle's possible association with a death or execution intend to belittle or downplay the circumstances of whoever may have suffered or died at the stockade.

Nick has just returned from a trip to Florida to visit a Fred B., the unit clerk from 1946 who had access to all the records. How can I contact him? Oddly, Nick doesn't remember his number, he says maybe Fred's in Bernandino or something like that. That's the best he can do. I decide, via an internet search, that it's San Fernandino, a small Florida beach town, and I call. After all, Nick's just been there, stirring up memories. An old man answers, curses, drops the phone; then an answering machine comes on.

Surely I've killed him.

A week later, after calling intermittently and still getting the machine, I try more numbers. On the third ring of the third number, someone answers with a gruff and wavery voice. He says he's Fred all right, and he knows Nick, but that's it. He's not talking.

Another vet tells me Fred has cancer everywhere; he

was ordered to watch the bombs go off at Los Alamos, give him a break.

"Move over, God, it's Mac." In 1944 MacArthur approved the execution of six young black soldiers for rape in New Guinea. As the commandant of the post, Walter Luszki was responsible for carrying out MacArthur's instructions to train and rehabilitate prisoners for return to duty as quickly as possible—and for the hangings. In *A Rape of Justice*, a book Luszki wrote fifty years later, he argues that the trial was full of irregularities, that there was no official awareness of the soldiers' sexual needs, and that MacArthur himself was a racist.

Luszki was the deputy chief provost marshal for GHQ in 1946 Tokyo.

It takes two weeks to get his book from interlibrary loan, a week to read it, two days to find Luszki's address, a day to write him a letter—and two weeks before someone calls to tell me he died two months earlier.

"We hanged twenty-two yanks in one morning," stated Harry "Kirky" Kirk, the English executioner for U.S. troops in Somerset. "They'd got people all over the place who been sentenced to death in this country and in Europe. . . . We did the lot in the one morning." When I ask Professor Lilly if these twenty-two were accounted for in the official numbers, he says no.

My son sits at a computer next to mine. He kills, vaporizes, slays one creature or anime character after another. "They're not real," he insists. Grossman, in *On Killing*, ends with a plea to curb children's use of these games, arguing that these are the ones that make killing possible, create that psychic distance, that quick wrist. No remorse.

The world can be that violent, generation after generation. Why practice?

"Mom," he says, "you're just afraid I'll be a desk fighter and work with the Predator, that remote-control plane that took down that al-Qaeda operative a couple of years ago."

He blows something up.

"Yeah," I say, "like that."

CHAPTER 21

The Japanese foliage is fluorescent green. I have always assumed that a shade this bright represented the idealized Japan, the lush forests and dewy moss being enjoyed seasonally, like the cherry blossoms. No. The foliage shines this color because it is either raining all the time, or the population is sweating, producing the humidity themselves.

Despite the day's downpour, we set out to do more street interviews, stopping first to talk to the proprietor of the local snack store just around the corner from Sherman's. Leaning over his wares, the man tells us he delivered food to the stockade—rice, vegetables, seafood, and potatoes—dragging the supplies on sledges because no one had cars. He insists that the MPs really liked the seaweed. He also tells us that two blocks away lived a large group of prostitutes in an area known as the Machiai. They had moved there for the stockade business because they knew the Americans were rich. Many of them "dated," but there were no marriages. After a throat-clearing Mifune noise, he shakes his head over my execution question. "The American police were frightening," he says, but now he knows that the Japanese are worse. He's seen them at riots with their rubber bullets, their intimidating helmets, their wall of shields.

A good-looking man walking a small dog accosts us. He'd seen us in the park interviewing and is anxious to talk. He was eight years old at the end of the war. The soldiers were very gentle, he remembers, and they gave him powdered milk. If they weren't so nice, they would have had more trouble from the locals, he says. They also threw gum and chocolate out of their jeeps when they drove around. Escaping prisoners made rope out of sheets, but they were arrested quickly be-cause they wore uni-

"A good-looking man walking a small dog."

forms that matched the severity of their crimes. (Hikaru notes that even prisoners are accorded status in the Japanese mind.) Some Japanese protected the escapees because they were sick or hungry, and they sympathized with them as underdogs. After all, the Japanese soldiers were underdogs, believing they could win the war with sharpened bamboo sticks, practicing on human shapes stuffed with straw.

Then he surprises us by saying that he estimates 85 percent of the Nakano residents had negative feelings about having a prison full of American criminals in their midst. The fact that they heard rumors about what went on inside only made them more frightened. After all, they couldn't tell who was a rapist or who was a murderer. He answers my question about executions by saying that any executions should have happened in the mainland United States. GIs and Japanese women? According to a cousin of his who worked as a prostitute at the American airfield, the women decided that each prostitute should have only one customer apiece in order to establish closer relationships and extract maximum benefits. Probably the same system worked for Nakano. As for him, he was just thankful that it was the Americans who came and not the North Koreans, who have so recently been showing off their nuclear missiles.

Private Eddie Slovik's execution made him World War II's most famous deserter. Executions for desertion are always made public, carried out to frighten the troops into obedience and also to show the folks back home that the army is doing its job. The Greeks and the Romans executed deserters for the same reason. Out of twenty-one thousand convicted deserters in World War II, Slovik was the one soldier chosen to set an example.

But he was a particularly sad choice. Born poor during the Depression, Slovik spent most of his boyhood in jail for petty thievery. He had just managed to go straight, get married, and hold down a job, when he was drafted. Experiencing the slaughter at the battlefield, he refused to shoot anyone and hid in a Canadian company.

It took Slovik fifteen minutes to die after the volley, even though they selected "the most combative types," because, as Grossman points out, the instinct against killing prevents even firing squads from being very accurate. Grossman argues that until the Vietnam War and its new psychological training strategies, soldiers throughout history avoided killing one another at all costs. "The U.S. Army Air Corps . . . discovered that during World War II less than 1 percent of their fighter pilots accounted for 30 to 40 percent of all enemy aircraft destroyed in the air, and . . . most fighter pilots 'never shot anyone down or even tried to.'" The army also discovered that "only 15 to 20 percent of the American riflemen in combat during World War II would fire at the enemy . . . they simply would not fire . . . even when faced with repeated waves of banzai charges," proving "the simple and demonstrable fact that there is within most men an intense resistance to killing their fellow man."

This reassures me.

Of course, after Slovik was killed, soldiers kept deserting. Execution has never proven to be a deterrent, in either military or civil life. But what an execution always produces is shame, which is why its records are hard to find. Author William Bradford Huie spent six years trying to extract information for *The Execution of Private Slovik,* and his was a very public trial.

We stop another old woman, who is stepping off a bridge to the street. To our surprise, she's someone we'd already approached when we were camped out at the supermarket. But she's happy to chat with Hikaru about her experiences in the north after the war. While they're talking, I see the man with the dog loitering nearby as if he too wants a repeat performance. Perhaps we've already interviewed all the people who are willing to talk.

We're debating whether to quit for the day, when Hikaru stops an elderly man in knee braces riding a bicycle. He looks at me instead of his translator when he says that the MPs put out their cigarettes in his vegetables, assuring him that the ash was good for the plants. He had been a soldier in New Guinea and used those bamboo sticks that they drilled with to kill animals, instead of Americans. After he returned, he often heard sirens from the stockade and saw the women walking around its perimeter. He referred to them as *panpan,* the obscenity my uncle used to call his dog. "Where there was need," the old man says, "the women went."

Sherman has one more idea for interviews. Despite his limited Japanese, he has been flirting with the women who work in the old-folks home near his house. They drive minivans rigged up with hot tubs for the elderly who don't have one at home. "These women must be in touch with someone who remembers what went on at the prison," says Sherman. But he's not charming enough—we don't get invited for a ride. We try the home itself. According to the young man in charge, no one there worked in the prison, but they would be happy to have us talk to them about their experiences living nearby.

Soon we are stepping out of an elevator into a room crammed with twenty-three old women sitting at tables. Here is where all the women are kept! We had found so few of them in the streets. A nurse walks between them to hand us a microphone. Hikaru is only briefly flustered, having spent some time working in television. She introduces me. I rack my brain for any scrap of Japanese to follow *konnichiwa*, "good afternoon," but all that comes out is English. They clap anyway.

Not many of the women look old enough to be put in a home, but one woman reveals she's ninety-eight—and that I look young for my age. A seventy-year-old woman with large glasses that make her eyes look weepy remembers running after the army's jeeps. A rhinestone-combed, blue-kimonoed woman in a wheelchair thought the American soldiers were so handsome. Another woman lived in Hiroshima at the time. We don't ask her opinion of Americans. An eighty-four-year-old woman in a wheelchair remembers American soldiers searching for Japanese women and the women running away and hiding and even holding on to trees so they wouldn't be taken. She thinks the American soldiers were weird and strange, having nothing better to do than chase Japanese women.

Before the interviews are finished, the staff at the

old-folks home starts removing the tables, realigning the chairs, explaining exercises. Perhaps we are upsetting the staff. The lights in the old women's faces go out while they concentrate on turning their ankles in unison. Just as we leave, a woman in a flowered shirt beckons to Hikaru. Her family had the local baths where the Japanese girls taught the GIs how to bathe.

"The Japanese had a long history of satisfying the instincts of foreign male guests," writes Burritt Sabin for the *Japan Times* in 2002.

The pleasure quarters in the 19th-century treaty ports had generally reserved a house for foreigners. However, the khakied and bell-bottomed bucks landing in Japan at the end of August [1945] were no 19th-century "guests." On the 28th, several hundred arrived at an R.A.A. [Recreation Amusement Association, houses of prostitution organized by the United States and Japan] facility under preparation in Omori, Tokyo. The sliding doors not yet in place, GIs and comfort women coupled in view of others.

Three days later, more than 100 GIs descended on Gorakuso, an apartment house in Yamashitacho, Yokohama, scheduled to open as an R.A.A. center on Sept. 1. "The facility opens tomorrow," explained an employee, whereupon a GI pointed a submachine gun at him. The GIs confined the employees. Then they set upon the 14 comfort women. One woman protested she would rather die than sleep with a black. Then, after she fled outdoors, stark naked, the spurned soldier caught her and beat her to death. He, in

turn, died at the hands of the military police. The
next morning the other women lay half-dead on
the floor where soldiers had trampled them."

"It is interesting to note that the subject of the very first
meeting between the top two military men of the U.S.
occupation forces immediately after the surrender ceremony was neither 'the democratization of Japan' nor
'the future status of Emperor Hirohito,' but 'rape by
Marines,'" according to Yuki Tanaka in *Japan's Comfort
Women: Sexual Slavery and Prostitution During World
War II and the U.S. Occupation.*

A huge black butterfly—so big I think at first it is a
hummingbird—visits each flowerpot, alighting and moving on. We are eating noodles outside a museum because
all the museums are closed today, closed not only on the
day of the festival, but the day after, another mysterious
Japanese custom. Just as mysterious as the existence of
this butterfly in super-tech downtown Tokyo. It swoops,
it hovers.

A white cat, so quick it's a blur, bats the butterfly out of the air. There's a chase. A tabby joins in. The
white one runs left, right while the big bug—I have to
deromanticize it—struggles. Is it eaten? The white cat
streaks away, the tabby sniffs the pot. No more butterfly.

I've never really considered the "Madame" in "Madame
Butterfly." She was just a tragic literary figure, Romeo's
Asian Juliet, the Japanese doll I received for Christmas
in 1958, not a woman who commits suicide because she
actually loves the American who so blithely leaves her.

In his memoir, *Time of Fallen Blossoms,* the Australian
officer Allan Clifton condemns the innkeeper's sister for
working as a madam until he notices four wooden boxes

in the entryway, which she tells him contain the ashes of her husband and children, killed in Hiroshima.

Before we return to the United States, Hikaru chooses to celebrate our stay in Japan at an Okinawan restaurant, giving us a literal taste of the antibase movement. Mulling over our interviews, I marvel at how easily people's claims to sovereignty and allegiance are swayed by their stomachs, with chocolate and gum, tobacco and potato peels. I imagine being hungry in that 1946 summer, the warmest in twenty years, possibly even as hot as this evening. But the restaurant is so air-conditioned, I quickly forget everything else but my own hunger.

As a farewell gesture, we compose *renga,* a collaborative Japanese poetry that, most simply, uses the last line of a poem for the first line of the next poem. We adjust the form further, collapsing it into the French game exquisite corpse, a pastime that sounds even more appropriate to my quest. Each of us writes two lines, covers the first, leaves the last to be expanded on by the next poet.

Lips move
Time passes
The clock laughs
I try laughing too
Even though bitten
It's only my legs
I have good new shoes
And like to walk
Chasing smoke down holes
Full of the past.

"Who are we? Where are we?" Sherman asks just before we part. "What does the pursuit of your uncle's story

mean to me and where has it got me? Do you want to clear
your uncle's name, or find something that clouds it?"

Tokyo offers me two stories:

Guards sleeping in the terrible X cells, looking out
on the devastated burnt landscape and into the gallows,
guards who loom over the occupied Japanese women as
well as the prisoners.

Or guards having the time of their lives, gallivanting
all over Tokyo with exotic, willing women, drinking beer
and fooling around, ignoring the prisoners.

What about the larger story, I argue with Sherman—
that of the executed men and their families? Of the be-
trayal of the military in not reporting what they had done?
What about sixty years later?

*When they saw us holding cigarettes out the windows,
they came running to the trains holding up fists full of
money. We bartered with them until the train started to
pull away, and we settled for the biggest wad of money.
We were not completely sure of all the different bills and
denominations so we just settled for volume. About the
third stop, we lucked into a new marketing skill, so to
speak. As the train started to pull out of the station during the exchange of cigarettes and money, I held onto
both of them. A sheer stroke of genius. By that afternoon, we had perfected this "exchange" so skillfully
that the three of us, bartering from our individual windows, had made a lot of money. When we lost all our
individual packages of cigarettes to superior grips or the
mistiming of the train departure, we stuffed the cartons
full of wood straw that was in the train seats. We eventually lost even the bogus cartons of cigarettes. That was
at nightfall. We sat around, laughing and joking, and
counting our money. We had parlayed six cartons of*

*cigarettes into about four thousand U.S. dollars. To put
that in perspective, that was more than our total pay as
a soldier for the three of us for one year.* [03/99]

Smoke, that's what I'm in pursuit of: Tokyo in ruins just
after the war, the Japanese valleys smoky with spray from
the crooked rivers, the smoky taste of summer sake clear
as water, all that cigarette smoke from the GI bars, the
smoky sex from the Japanese *panpan* girls with their
long red fingernails, my uncle's smoking thievery, the
smoke of the 1973 fire in the National Archives, which
burned all the records of so many military men and their
mistakes, the smoke of cremation, how bodies disappear
when they can't be buried, and the smoke of silence, of
words unsaid.

I wiggle my fingers through all that smoke and that's
it, history.

IV

The MP Museum repeats that they have no record of the existence of the 483rd military police escort guard. The National Archives online search agrees. "But my uncle stated the number twice in his memoir. Very clearly," I say to the slightly mustached and very harried archivist I meet at the National Archives (NARA) in College Park, Maryland. "Are you sure, you know—was he in his right mind?" The archivist turns away from his computer. He has pressed me for details, any clues that might help narrow my search. It is his job to press. I have foolishly told him all I know, I have used the words *suicide* and *executions*. At best he thinks I'm a sensationalist, at worst a crazy weirdo. But I'm neither, I'm like 85 percent of the people there, someone who wants information about a relative; I'm just after a few facts my taxes have paid to have archived.

"This part of the tape he'd completed several years before his depression," I tell him.

"And you're writing a novel?"

"Memoir," I say.

He proceeds to say that novels tend to show things in the wrong light. "Why, when I was a detective," he begins. And tells me about the time his partner tried to slide his gun out of his holster during a stakeout and it went down his pant leg. "Something like that can get blown way out of proportion in your memory," he says. "It wasn't funny at all at the time."

The clock behind him says 2:00. I have two more hours of my two-day search before the place closes. I sense he's stonewalling, that he thinks I have a subject too flimsy to pursue. I have not yet piqued his archival urge, the sleuth that stirs in the heart of all reference librarians.

He escorts me back into the reading room. I try to shake his hand, but other researchers already surround him. He hurries off.

I find, deep within the army's records, a notice that the 483rd was reviewed in 1946. After I fetch the archivist by name, he scans the document, pulls another binder from the shelf, nods, and finds a citation that could confirm the first. "You won't have time to request this—the last pull has already gone out," he says.

The look on my face.

"Come," he tells me.

We exit the waiting room, we take two turns around what must be a pentagon-shaped foyer and then an elevator. A pair of blindfolds would have confused me less. We go down of course, down, down, down. After a series of corridors there is Kafka heaven: as far as I can see, rows of gray document boxes stacked to the ceiling on racks.

I tell him I used to be a rare-manuscript curator, that I hated getting pricked by all the rusty straight pins holding the ancient letters and documents together. "I was afraid of contracting tetanus," I say. He doesn't comment. No doubt I sound even more implausible.

We turn left, we turn right, we walk down an aisle. He heaves a box off the shelf and plucks out a file.

That's how easy it could be.

The file says that the 483rd changed from an escort

guard into a company in 1951 at Camp McCoy. That's it. Months later I discover a 483rd unit assigned to a secret area in Nevada in the 1960s. Months after that, I find out that the reason I can't track my uncle's unit is because in Japan it was temporarily renamed Headquarters and Headquarters, a no-name, handy if you don't want soldiers to have a reunion.

Now that I know the unit number, I can contact his buddies. To find their names I have to order a morning report from the National Personnel Records Center in St. Louis. By mail, no faxes, no phone calls. It will take months to process and will only show changes in the roll, not everyone. Then I have to find them.

I complete the form. I still have an hour at the Archives. My request for the court-martial ledger has been filled.

I turn its thick extra-long pages, the military's Domesday-looking book of the sentenced. I check the capital offenses, rape and murder. Prisoners are listed by the number of their courts-martial, not by names or service numbers. Later I find out that there's another set of volumes I can search for court-martial numbers via their names, but even if I have the name, they are never in alphabetical order. Now, paging through the book, I fill with despair. The column that should show the final disposition of any of the postwar condemned—Hanged—is stamped B. O. C. in red, red ink.

The archivist doesn't know what that means for the condemned. The librarian I call at the Judge Advocate General library in Charlottesville, Virginia, doesn't know either. The U.S. American Military History Institute guesses "Board of Corrections," which doesn't get me any closer to what happened.

MacArthur must have known. He had to sign the papers. "We don't have anything," says the MacArthur archivist.

"And forget General Willoughby, MacArthur's chief intelligence officer, the one with the Japanese mistress. He was a burner."

"More smoke."

More smoke.

"Sentences of death . . . must be confirmed by the President. There are important exceptions to this, however, in time of war," according to the House Committee on Military Affairs. Is an occupation part of a war? Certainly in Iraq it is considered so. Even if the Japanese weren't fighting the American occupiers, their land was militarily controlled. What is a war? Why was the committee equivocating in 1946?

MPs don't like to keep records, the archivist tells me.

"MPs don't like to keep records."

The archivists do not stonewall the second time I visit. I'm allowed to copy the Eighth Army stockade's Return of General Prisoners for the months my uncle served. Although my uncle said he was guarding a crowded six hundred prisoners, in an average month no more than one hundred appear on these rolls. The Eastern State Penitentiary held seven hundred prisoners, so his estimate makes sense. Setting aside that confusion, these reports show a lot of crossing out, which the archivist says to ignore, even the two "corrected reports" during the most crowded months. Could the silent clerk from San Fernandino have been the one to have done the crossing out?

But even ignoring these deadly-looking Xs, the reports are exciting—James Chisholm is obviously the "Jism" my uncle mentioned, the prisoner whose conduct is consistently rated "bad." I find two of the three "Greens" my uncle talked about. Captain Millar, with an "a," signs the reports. I couldn't have known the spelling from just listening to tapes. Then, the month after the prison list diminishes, Captain Millar becomes Major Millar and moves on. *The captain accomplishes what he sets out to do.*

"I find two of the three 'Greens.'"

But no one is condemned to death. Even Hicswa's sentence is listed as twenty-five years.

There must be a mistake. I reread all of them.

No mistake.

But the guards were told they held prisoners with the death sentence. Such misinformation must have terrified the prisoners, expecially being kept in Japan, so far from anywhere they could get help.

I find an April report from the 483rd MPs—does a unit have to be triangulated to exist?—that says that the stockade is getting too crowded, and there's a later report from the 720nd MP unit, who are ordered to loan forty MPs to the stockade because of the restless attitude of the prisoners. In November the inspector general still refers to an excess of sixty-two prisoners.

Still no prison breaks are noted in any of the reports, and no deaths. Another file says all the prisoners were shipped to Camp McQuaide, in California. Neither the archives nor the military has records of Camp McQuaide. The internet reveals that the Seventh-Day Adventists bought the military's oceanside location in 1948. I imagine the executed prisoners shipped there in boxes, the receipts for these boxes burned by the army with the rest of the trash from the abandoned base. Or would I just find more files like one marked Burial—Court-Martialed Military Personnel, with its single sheet of paper covered with coded numbers and letters, the meaning of which no one now remembers?

Then the prisoners' personnel information begins to arrive from National Personnel Records Center in St. Louis. Chisholm and two others were discharged in Japan, another was discharged in the Philippines. The West Point major I call to find out whether criminals were ever released in the country of incarceration says that would never be done; two other servicemen concur. The date of discharge for the troublemaker Chisholm coincides with a document requesting that he spend seven days in isolation. All of the men are listed to sail for Camp McQuaide during the same period.

"I have kept asking myself," writes W. G. Sebald, ". . . what the invisible connections that determine our lives are, and how the threads run."

"Mom," says my son, "you never strategize." We're trying to play checkers, but I'm hopeless. I see a good spot and I just move, time after time. Sometimes I win—I'm good at improvising. He used to complain that he couldn't figure out what I was planning. Now he knows better: I don't.

I am too straightforward, I ask exactly what I need to know. "You can't be too broad in topic for librarians or they think you haven't done the research, and you can't be too narrow or they can't help you. And above all, don't scare them," cautions my wonderful Fordham reference librarian. The ancient, most senior archivist at the National Archives suggests paying a researcher to do the work. I'm suspicious about handing over money to someone who's so close to their system that the archivist has his phone number; theirs is a system that can't seem to find anything unless I find it myself. Left in the reference section on a third visit, I pull down enough books to find a citation that lo and behold yields a misfiled file labeled Executions. It confirms the "lost" Pentagon list and adds another five executions, but the only man executed in 1946 was in the European theater.

The National Archives' protocol—I slide a card through a reader, I open my computer for inspection, I hand over every piece of paper for their official stamp, I sign in and out of all the rooms with my badge and number dangling from my neck, I keep some trolleys and some I must return, all the while constantly under electronic surveillance, including the clicking tiny spy camera the researcher next to me uses on his documents—their elaborate game of security, certainly doesn't suggest that the files were stolen. A much simpler act of misfiling hides a document forever, effectively destroying it.

Nonetheless, I am elated to unearth that Executions file, verifying the Pentagon list. Someone kept track. Then I'm depressed. I realize that probably there were no "secret" executions, that the military just doesn't want me to find out about them. That is to say, it's not as if they don't have records in triplicate, just like all the others, stapled and screwed and pinned into the files; it's that they are filed somewhere special. I've seen the file where MacArthur asks the provost marshal to send him radio reports of anyone sentenced to be executed. Someone must have kept those. But no, says his archivist. All we have are reports of sentencing, no reports of executions.

Three people could have commuted a death sentence: a commanding officer, MacArthur, and Truman.

The Harry S. Truman Library has no record of a 1946 execution in Japan. Hicswa was Truman's only pardon that year.

President Lincoln granted a record 331 clemency warrants during his time in office. General Sherman found a way to deal with his leniency. When someone inquired of the general how he was able to execute court-martialed soldiers without Lincoln granting them pardons, he said, "I shot them first."

What records I do find contradict themselves. Documents sent to me by the National Personnel Records Center show the wrong length of service; the dates correspond with the court-martial, not the day of release—or sometimes not. How can anyone believe that the three documents showing that men were released in Japan are any more reliable than those that show they were shipped away, when I find other papers that show no one stayed in Japan? The interviewer of the chief jailor mentions that executed war criminals in Europe were cremated and their ashes thrown in the river.

Smoke.

I am not good at commandeering help. I ask for help helplessly. I am not a journalist on a paid mission of neutrality. I will blow stories out of proportion because I'm in love with my subject, the only possible explanation for my doggedness.

"Smoke."

In January 1946, my uncle is one of 64,846 replacements.

A week later, reviewing all the Google entries I made over the last year, I find a working email from the Sugamo Prison reunion site. William M.'s response is as suspicious as Billy F.'s wife's. *Why would I talk to you, a total stranger?* This, in turn, makes me suspicious. Vets are usually eager to recall their histories. I email him with credentials and a summary of my interests, leaving out the executions, my uncle's suicide, not wanting to bring up trauma. I wait.

He emails back:

> The gallows were still there in a warehouse building behind cell block #2, next to an entrance way into the prison designated as "the motor pool gate." Cell block #7 was the area where all prisoners serving from 10 years to life or death were incarcerated. If one's death sentence were to be carried out the individual would be moved from his cell in block 7 to a cell in block 2 and kept under "close custody" until the death warrant was carried out.

He volunteers that he was there for an execution of a murderer in 1949. Two of his buddies remember it too. Since this happened after the initial chaos of the occupation, he agrees that there is no excuse for the lack of records. He's the one who remembers that the widow took the body home; no one was left buried in Japan. "You had to pay a yearly fee to keep your burial spot, and if you didn't pay, out you went."

I receive the morning reports. Now what? I google a few names and get close to nowhere. I refuse any of the costly background checks and despair. Then I find Ancestry.com, their extensive military records and their tantalizing "Living People Finder." Armed with phone numbers, I leave a message on another of the ex-guards' machines. His wife calls back, suspicious about how I found his name. Her main question is, however, whether I am with the "extreme left wing" that wants to discredit military prisons since Abu Ghraib. I parry with my uncle's suicide. She relents a little, suggests that I call on Saturdays or Mondays, her husband's days off. Should I ask him what his mental condition is? Over eighty, he still works part-time. When I reach him, he tells me he found Japan very interesting, but does not want to talk about guarding, about solitary, the gallows, or executions. He doesn't remember a thing, he just wants to know how I found him.

February 2, '46

Four Negroes made a prison break 2 nights ago,
took a stove poker and made a hook out of it
and tied a rope to it and hooked it in the wall.
Found them in a geisha house about a block
away. They are in solitary now.

Black prisoners desperate to escape—just for sex?

On July 4 two years after my uncle's breakdown, I realize I have to disregard the psychiatrist's warning about traumatizing the vets if I'm ever going to find out what was going on. My promise to my uncle to write the book must take precedent. So many more veterans have died by now that I can't afford to hesitate. I will ask each of them if it's okay to talk, knowing so clearly the pain it has caused in my own family.

I reach four MPs in the Northwest. All of them pause when I ask about the gallows, the executions. Chan M. is quick to tell me that he made so much money—even sold his beer—during his eighteen-month stint that he bought a Caterpillar tractor when he returned home. The "geisha house" he remembers as great fun. End of conversation. No eighty-year-old vet is going to regale me with stories about his whirl with prostitutes on the phone.

I decide to use Hicswa, the stockade's most famous prisoner, to keep them talking. Chan thinks Hicswa was a little ornery. Ben remembers Hicswa terrifying him by hiding under his bed. The captain told the guards that they would have to serve the prisoner's sentence if a prisoner escaped, and Ben certainly didn't want Hicswa's. (So that's what my uncle risked!) Marvin B., the cook, doesn't remember Hicswa at all. One of his Japanese helpers put a pepper shaker in front of a fan as a joke, he tells me, but alas, he remembers nothing about an educated Japanese kitchen assistant who might have challenged my uncle to a judo match. He reminds me that the soldiers lived in the X cells.

Otis H. in Idaho wants to talk while he is on dialysis. He worked in the stockade infirmary and remembers that one guy they had for a while didn't know what unit he was in. I am thrilled—it had to have been my uncle, after his helmet exploded in the guardhouse. But of course Otis has no idea who it was anymore. He remembers becoming quite friendly with the black prisoners who had formed a singing group, and when he left, they had just started building the gallows.

Eugene R. played football with the Yokohama Sixth Army before transferring to the stockade. He remembers that they built the gallows inside between cell blocks and that it should've been built outside, and that it had a ninety-pound trapdoor on it. He "walked the wall" around the stockade as a guard and remembers at least two escapes. A Lieutenant Glass there might have been "a little rough" with the prisoners, he says. He'd slept on guard duty too.

"I just couldn't stay awake." He sounds quite cautious by the time the conversation ends.

Theodore M. was the prison-supply sergeant who played the guitar and drove a jeep up Mt. Fuji. He remembers Hicswa as a "strange little dude." There were indeed no windows in solitary, and black curtains hung all around the gallows.

I am buoyed after speaking to Theodore, whose energy seems to come from his third wife, a stewardess he met through the *Oprah Winfrey Show*. He remembers the gallows and the bunting, Hicswa, and even mentions that Captain Millar might have worn glasses. But nothing about executions.

When my husband bought a pair of shoes for our trip to Tokyo at Eastern Mountain Sports, his salesman mentioned that Irv D., the old guy who worked there, was an MP in Japan around that time, but that he'd called in sick that day.

I was sure he was dying, but when I called the store the next day, he was the one who answered. He'd been with EMS since it opened and regaled me in his high-pitched voice with stories of 1946 Hokkaido and what it was like as a sergeant to drive the provost marshal's car and have everyone salute, something they didn't do now for him at EMS. He doubted that any executions occurred at the stockade because soldiers then were so gossipy. A day after all the residents of Hokkaido turned in their guns, all 750 of them, a colonel telegrammed from the south, hundreds of miles away, and ordered the only wooden-handled pistol they had confiscated to be sent to him as a souvenir.

But if the men were so chatty, why had they not heard

about the gallows that even A. G. Corey, the Korean War vet I interviewed first, remembers from passing through the stockade in 1952?

"All autobiographical memory is true; it is up to the interpreter to discover in which sense, where [and] for which purpose," writes Luisa Passerini, famed oral historian.

CHAPTER 24

May 4, '46

Dearest 1

Just missed a big chance to stay in Japan for 3 years. I've been in court the last 2 days on an armed robbery charge. The 720 MP picked me up with a couple extra watches, some extra, extra yen and a 45, which in this stage of occupation is not the proper thing to wear but my service record was clear and my CO being the prisoner officer cleared me of the charges.

Was it just the luck of race that prevented my uncle from being tossed into the prison himself? Such a close call should have made him more sympathetic to the plight of the prisoners. "The sentry is almost certain to have more human feelings for a prisoner whom he guards all day than for an officer whom he salutes once a week," writes L. D. Hankoff in *The Military Prison: Theory, Research and Practice,* a collection of essays on prison guards.

I need to talk to the ex-prisoners. There's no morning report for them, just the Monthly Return of General Prisoners. I research the ninety-eight prisoners who have odd names on Ancestry.com. John Doe is safe from my scrutiny because he has too many listings, but so is Emmit Gray; there were six men with that name born about the same time in the same part of the South. Several times men of the same name, presumably cousins, enlist from different counties. Most of the ex-prisoners are Southerners.

Their names tend to reoccur in their grandchildren; the ex-prisoners' names sometimes appear on the internet after their offspring have themselves been arrested. A handful of prisoners don't appear at all, which means their births, deaths, social-security numbers, cars, and houses have never been registered. Maybe they changed their names. The most common employment put down on the enlistment papers of the young men—no matter what state they come from—is lumberjack or geographer or oboe player. Who was the smart aleck at headquarters who unilaterally ordered this nomenclature? A twenty-year-old black man from Georgia is listed as having been "a motion picture director." Two or three of the prisoners die in Korea, out of the hundred who were eventually "volunteered" from the stockade—that is, given the choice of risking their lives on the battlefield or continuing to serve their time. When at last I find a few phone numbers, they are often disconnected, and more than once, someone answers and tells me: *Been dead for close to five years now.* I'm chasing Death itself.

So many more ex-prisoners are dead than MPs, although they're very close to the same age. The few prisoners who do answer usually hang up, or a gruff voice tells me even if he were home, he's not interested in talking or he doesn't want whatever I'm selling. The one ex-prisoner who finally talks is forced-jolly with me, saying he was an MP like my uncle and that he served in Yokohama. But he doesn't know anything about the Eighth Army stockade, no, sorry. It isn't that he doesn't remember the gallows, he doesn't remember anything at all. I say it must've been fun in Yokohama and he agrees; he does remember that he "had a great time." It is only after I put the phone down that I see that he was indeed an MP—in the stockade for larceny.

. . .

What the ex-prisoners from the Eighth Army stockade
can't guess is that by corroborating my uncle's details,
they might release to the families of the prisoners the true
story of what happened—and perhaps give up their guilt
for remaining silent.
In the novel *Stockade,* the defense counsel Captain
Colby also finds it hard to get prisoners to talk about
abuse, abuse so severe in the novel that more than one
of them dies.

"What about all those prisoners and ex-prisoners
we interviewed?" Captain Colby asked. "Black
and Hamish aren't going to smell so sweet after
they testify to some of the things that went on
under Black's administration . . ."
"I wouldn't waste time with the men who
are still in the stockade," [his assistant says]. "I
interviewed about a dozen of them and gave up.
They're not going to take a chance on lousing
themselves up!"
. . . .
"What about the others, Larry?" . . . .
"We can't count on them either. You know
what I said about ex-cons being allergic to cops
and courtrooms."

It's a game of hangman, each shred of evidence—how
shred conjures up a machine chewing up documents!—
nailed to an armature until it resembles a body. I search
for weeks for several prisoners my uncle mentioned by
name as particularly difficult and who therefore, I reason,
might have been up for execution or at least might bear a
grudge and want to talk—until I realize I should be looking for prisoners with excellent records; they would be

the ones most likely to have survived, the least likely to have been executed.

In *Who Owns Death?* Robert Jay Lifton and Greg Mitchell interview prosecutors, judges, jurors, and wardens about their experiences sentencing prisoners, guarding the condemned, and seeing them executed. They outline the possibility of their experiencing severe post-traumatic stress disorder, sometimes occurring many years later. They quote Donald Cabana, author of the memoir *Death at Midnight: The Confession of an Executioner.* "It didn't matter that Starkweather was one of the most hated men of the decade. They say the warden never got over it."

Today prisons have begun using lethal injection to protect the witnesses required at executions from trauma. Although witnessing the death is important both from the standpoint of the gravity of taking a person's life and of proving that the state can take a life and thereby use execution as a method of deterrence, it produces a voyeurism that implicates the witnesses as well—they too become executioners because they do nothing to prevent it.

Before Ivan Turgenev attended the beheading of a Parisian murderer in 1870, he repeated to himself, "I have no right, I have no right." He felt that "by being present with an air of hypocritical solemnity at the killing of a being like us, we are participating in some kind of lawless detestable farce." Fyodor Dostoyevsky was nearly executed himself and insisted that "the attributes of the executioner are to be found in almost every contemporary man," a comment that the Zimbardo study certainly proves true. According to Lifton and Mitchell, Tolstoy's response to witnessing an execution was that "all politics [were] a lie and . . . he would 'never serve any government, anywhere.'"

CHAPTER 25

"We had finished corn harvest that year," says Dad. "And we didn't have much welding to do over the winter. It was the early sixties. Do you remember? We laid the boy off. We didn't have any repair work left because we had bought new equipment, a big new tractor, bought mostly from the bank."

We'd been talking about guns. A preternaturally gifted teenage friend of my sister's children had killed himself with a gun recently. "It was because of the gun," says Dad. "And this kid back then was a nice kid too, maybe because his dad was so hard on him, but maybe that made him good to work with. Anyway, he went home after we told him he was laid off and stuck a gun in his mouth and killed himself. You remember that? You were in high school at the time."

"I think I was in grade school." I slowly roll up my window. "All I remember is that his father, who ran the hardware store, rented a merry-go-round every year and set it up in his parking lot for the Catholic-school kids."

"I guess you would remember that." Dad isn't looking at me, he's driving, showing off his crops. A farmer likes nothing better than to check the height of his corn, the weed situation, the fences. He's trying to tell me something else his way, obliquely, in a kind of blur like the crops we pass so quickly.

"The kid did it because there was a gun in the house," he says. "If he had gone home and found no gun around or ammo, he couldn't have shot himself. He wasn't old enough to buy one."

"And your brother?"

"My brother had everything. Nothing wrong with that." Dad stops and studies his corn. "We told the boy there wasn't any more work right then. He was a good worker. He was unhappy about it."

Dad drives on to review the handsome French sunflowers he's planted in the next section. They are turned toward us. Really they are turned toward the sun, and bowed because the sun is too much to bear.

I once wrote a story about that suicide. As in real life, in the story I was twelve and wore a single long braid that I whipped around my head while riding the merry-go-round, hoping that the man's son would see me. He had muscles—I realize now, built up from working for Dad—but he was going steady with a girl whose mother long ago my father almost married. It was fall, when farm communities do their buying. Maybe the merry-go-round brought customers. In my story, it's the father who commits suicide. I'd completely forgotten that it was the son. Did I change the story out of guilt, thinking that by trying to attract his attention with my whipping braid, I had somehow caused his suicide?

Guilt, with its centrifugal force.

I hadn't known Dad's part in the boy's suicide at all.

Old men with guns have the highest rate of suicide, higher than that of teenagers.

Two and a half years after my uncle's death, my aunt sends me two photos from his time in Japan. He doesn't look six-three with his bulky khakis tucked into his boots in the first picture, and he looks sweaty. His swagger is tentative, appropriate for a kid who has survived being blown out of his post in an explosion and then later hit in the head so hard in a race riot he spends eighteen days in the hospital, a race riot he mentions casually in one of his last letters home at the end of the year. In the second photo, a shorter buddy hangs off his shoulder, looking plastered, a mess tin dangling from his hand. My uncle has more of a smile this time and his big high school ring is evident, the one he embossed the sailor's forehead with. You can't see his muscles under his jacket, but he must have them. The most amazing thing is that it's the first time I've ever seen him without his black glasses.

A journalist reporting on female soldiers in Iraq tells me the glasses are called BCGs. Officially, "basic corrective glasses"—but they are so ugly the soldiers always call them birth-control glasses.

Clark Kent kept his on.

CHAPTER 26

June 4, '46

Tokyo Japan

As you see by the new address I have changed abodes once again. We had another prison break and it being my luck I shot one of the prisoners. They court martialled me, gave me a carton of cigarettes and a transfer.

I am stunned by his admission—of course, it doesn't say he killed the man, he could still be telling the truth in his memoirs about not killing anyone, but the insouciance, the jokey casualness, of the *carton of cigarettes* suggests the worst.

Despite the average boy's seeing sixteen thousand TV murders before he's eighteen and hundreds in the ninety minutes of almost any first-run movie, he won't have any idea what it's really like to kill one person close-up. Grossman writes that the Hollywood depiction of killing someone is about as real as the pornographic-movie version of the sexual experience. "A virgin observer might get the mechanics of sex right by watching an X-rated movie, but he or she could never hope to understand the intimacy and intensity of the procreative experience." After discussing bayoneting, machine gunning, and aerial bombing, he states that the hardest, most traumatic way to kill someone is face-to-face.

. . .

"The bad guys aren't anyone special, they just appear," says my son. "You know they're bad because they're running away. You always shoot them in the back. If they turn around, you're dead."

"We have six times more prisoners than anybody else in the world," I say, wandering away from my own screen. "Probably six times more computer-game players than anywhere else in the world too."

"A faster connection can fix a lot of things," laughs my son, banging on the keys. "Hey, you know it's not all Predator fighting in Iraq. They do a lot of hand-to-hand."

"Great. That should make post-traumatic stress even worse."

"I don't know about that," says my son. He doesn't look up. "Don't distract me."

You're reflected in their eyes, you're the last person they see. They take your image into their deaths, and you take theirs. Whether accidental or purposeful, such a death must haunt the survivor. Did my uncle kill himself because he couldn't talk about it? So what if it wasn't Omaha Beach. Trauma doesn't compare. After my four-year-old fell out a window, another parent told me how much worse it was for him, with a nineteen-year-old. Trauma is trauma.

"A prisoner got out of line and grabbed my brother's gun while he was guarding the chow line," repeats Dad. "He wrestled him down and the gun went off."

I imagine the intimacy of it: the face next to my uncle's, the gush of blood in the embrace, the hot breath of the last words. Face-to-face.

"But he wasn't supposed to have a gun inside the stockade. It must've happened outside, maybe he did shoot prisoner Number Six while he was clearing brush?"

I can practically hear Dad shake his head on the phone, not no or yes, but as if shaking off the question. "You know, he came out to see me branding cattle and gave me a big hug. He must've already made up his mind about the suicide." Dad clears his throat. "I wanted to go down to see him in Texas earlier, but I didn't."

"I only know what he told me."

"Maybe he didn't want company. He didn't want mine."

"Maybe. I only know what he told me."

The idea of hand-to-hand trauma is so persuasive I put trauma by execution to one side. Besides, the file on military executions is restricted and my Freedom of Information Act request to see it has been pending for two years. Without a name, I have to examine every court-martial on record. Then the NARA archivist gives me another version of the court-martial ledgers filed under the same number, and I find execution dates written in a lovely feminine hand replacing the uninformative bloody red stamp B.O.C. But not all of them are resolved with a stay or a hanging, and where the executions took place isn't noted.

I find no record of my uncle's three courts-martial.

The military had "short holdings," informal or summary hearings that were not recorded, regarding irregularities on duty. I would have thought the wounding or killing of a prisoner might warrant a full investigation, but ex-guard Vincent M. isn't surprised. "That's what we were there for, to threaten them with guns."

He's one of the guards listed on my last morning report, the one with MPs I hadn't contacted. I didn't want to call any more of them—guards or prisoners. They never want to talk to me and whatever they say only hammers home how wrongheaded my uncle was to suggest there were executions.

But I have to.

Two are dead, two numbers are disconnected, but I talk to six more. Vincent is the best. *That name sounds familiar,* he says in a silky Sinatra voice, and it's like a fairy tale he remembers so much. He remembers my uncle as "the guy who earned a black belt while he was there." He also remembers two prisoners besides Hicswa waiting for the gallows. He says one of them "was a colored boy who was sleeping with a Japanese girl who decided to scream *rape.*" Then Leroy S. remembers that they did execute at least one prisoner and sent his body back to the States. Jack W. remembers too. I reach Jack even though his name is badly garbled in the morning report. Then John J. says his room had a view of the gallows and that he could see when the rope went taut.

Oh, my god. Not only was there at least one execution, but it is possible that my uncle really did wake up and see a hanging body! If one soldier saw it, so could another, from a different angle—I didn't dream up the whole thing myself. Holding my breath, I ask, *And did you ever see that rope go taut?* He says yes, just once. That colored boy.

Only blacks were executed for rape in England, and a year later, only blacks—six men—were hanged for rape by MacArthur in New Guinea.

Incidents of rape in Japan went out of control in spring 1946. Because one in four GIs had VD, MacArthur had been forced to completely reverse his stance on "butterflying" and make prostitution and fraternization illegal. But his decree backfired. In *Embracing Defeat,* John Dower says that "the number of rapes and assaults on Japanese women amounted to around 40 *daily* while R. A. A. was in operation, and then rose to an average of 330 a day after it was terminated in early 1946." Those were the reported rapes. Two incidents of mass rape from that time period were so outrageous they were also reported: on April 4, fifty GIs broke into a hospital in the Omori district and raped seventy-seven women, even a woman who had just given birth, killing a two-day-old baby by tossing it onto the floor; and on April 11, forty U.S. soldiers cut off the phone lines of one of Nagoya's city blocks and entered a number of houses simultaneously, "raping many girls and women between the ages of 10 and 55 years." By May 1946 MacArthur had a huge problem with rape. What better solution than to make an example of "the colored boy?"

Japanese workmen completed building the gallows and soldiers tested them in May 1946. My uncle was transferred out at the end of May. The clerk/typist for that month is the one who refuses to be interviewed.

I dive back into my papers. Melvin Mossberg is the only prisoner listed as convicted of rape in the month of May, but his name certainly sounds more Jewish than black. I find him on the prisoners' roster through June, although his official record shows that he was discharged January 18, 1946. Is he listed as shipped to Camp McQuaide in July?

He is. But there are no records to say he arrived.

Richard S., another clerk/typist for the stockade, remembers an escape in which a prisoner ripped the front off a paperback and wrote on the first page: *I'll be back when I have some fun*—and he was. Richard's friend at the prison, another MP named Sergeant Kimmel, committed suicide right after he returned home.

Where did Sergeant Kimmel sleep? How close to the prisoners did he get? What Japanese woman did he hold in his arms? Did no one understand his pain when he returned? I find Burnum W. Kimmel on the same list as the five men who remember the hanging. I would like to make something of his suicide, another "veteran haunted by executions kills self," but that would be irresponsible. I know nothing more, it's just a coincidence. It's just something.

The ex–provost marshal John C., someone who might be responsible, says he was sent home two weeks too soon, at the very beginning of the most mysterious month of May. He remembers nothing about a gallows. Perhaps he was considered too softhearted to order an execution: he was one of the rare military men who objected to the bombing of Hiroshima and Nagasaki, having seen afterward how inadequate the Japanese defenses were. He doesn't visit either site during his tenure. He does, however, recall my uncle's name, but can't remember the context.

Another guard, Larry S., mentions that he witnessed a prisoner going for a guard's shoulder holster—and that the guard shot him to death. Was that my uncle? "It happened all the time," says Larry.

The last guard I call, Roger H., remembers the gallows but will not talk about it; he cuts the conversation short. "People did get shot once in a while," he says. "It was a prison."

It has been three years since Abu Ghraib. I think the vets have forgotten about it, just as the military hopes, which might account for why they are so much more forthcoming and suddenly remember the gallows and its use.

Oral historian Luisa Passerini interviewed the women of Turin twenty years after World War II. Each woman was interviewed separately, yet all of them had a hole in their histories: the time when their husbands were lined up and shot to death.

I find this:

"During the late 1940s and 1950s, a GI mistress was known as an '*onrii*,' from the English 'only one,'" writes Michael S. Molasky.

> This was a more prestigious position among prostitutes. Not only did it provide greater security, an apartment or house, and make fewer demands on the body, but it occasionally led to marriage— although far less often than was promised. As

opposed to an "only," a prostitute who accepted multiple customers was sometimes referred to as a "butterfly."

Technically, my uncle didn't "know" the butterfly. Only the *onrii*. He was a good Midwestern boy, settling down with one woman, marrying her.

If he left before Kyochan delivered, maybe she did visit the shrine for aborted babies, with its little red-caped and bibbed statues so conveniently located nearby, and then moved on to the next customer, or relocated to the nearby air base. Or maybe she kept the baby. A prostitute with many clients must have to divorce her feelings, but what about a woman with a single partner? Maybe she loved him.

The scenario cannot be so easily drained of feeling.

In the 1956 film *The Man in the Gray Flannel Suit*, Gregory Peck's struggle up the corporate ladder is interrupted by flashbacks from the World War II trenches in Italy and love scenes of an adulterous liaison. He makes good on the resulting war baby by sending the Italian woman money, but the act almost destroys his marriage. Peck is his most wooden in this film—the zeitgeist then was all about no emotion!—but I wonder how influential his performance was. After seeing it, did men rush to the courts to support their bastards abroad? Did my uncle leap upon his tractor and smite the corn?

I drive through the car-dealership sprawl in central Texas to my cousin Chris's little town. It sits at the start of hill country, with antique shops in converted old railroad stations—or is it stagecoach stops?—an outdoor amphitheater with stone seats, and mounting crests of bed-and-breakfasts situated along a beautiful creek. It isn't Nebraska but the air is dry, the birds come in flocks, and there is a faint smell of manure in the air when the wind is right. An older development encircles a golf course where my cousin's house stands, its front door piled high with self-addressed boxes from Nebraska. No one answers the door, but I've heard from her husband's secretary that my cousin is out of town for medical treatment. Here on a last-minute business trip, I am just hoping she's come home early and I can catch her in. No such luck.

Across a little creek on their property stands a grove of pines around a neat glass-fronted shed with a large image of Buddha seated inside, surely where my uncle tried to learn to meditate. Just twenty-six miles away is Fort Hood, the largest military installation in the United States. The tank-training ground booms with exploding ordnance.

"Why isn't the book finished?" Dad says on the phone a year after his brother's suicide.

"Dad," I say, "it isn't just typing."

"I know—you're like Frank Lloyd Wright. When he had the commission for Fallingwater, he procrastinated. Finally his client called and said he was coming to look at the plans. Wright knew he was at least four hours away, in some remote part of—where? Pennsylvania? By the time the client arrived, he had the sketches all drawn out."

"I'll bet it took him months to deliver the plans and a year or more to build the house."

"I'm just trying to understand how you work."

I'm flattered, I should have said. Dad's never taken an interest before. "I'll send you the transcripts of the tapes," I offer instead.

"I want to see it all laid out in a book," he says. "So people will believe he wasn't just tired of life, that it was something else."

What if that something else makes him not Superman, I don't say.

I click the cassette player on and off, hearing *Abu, Abu,* on that otherwise blank side.

It's after midnight, fall 2006, and I'm lost on the grounds of the U.S. Army War College in Carlisle, Pennsylvania.

My taxi zipped away as soon as I found an address vaguely similar to the one on my printout and now I'm dragging my luggage through the leaves blowing across the sidewalks, with no one to ask for directions. Of course there's no public phone and I don't carry a cell phone—but anyway, whom can I call? All the little look-alike houses on their curving roads sit dark, and no dogs lurk. I cross onto what appears to be a park, past a gazebo—"reviewing the troops" comes to mind—toward a crack of light in a white-pillared Southern-style mansion. I tap on the window. The general is up, though he's not a general, he's just a major doing research at the library like me, and he's about to walk the dog. Of course he'll show me the way. We chat about the ironies of the place, how in the midnineteenth century, it trained Indian fighters, only to educate Native American children a few years later. The next morning, I walk past the tombstones of the 190 Native American children who died here of forced assimilation complicated by TB or influenza.

My uncle was a sophisticated man. Why would he think that stories about the occupation, without a single battle or confrontation other than those due to his own pugnaciousness, would be worthy of publication, let alone a major motion picture? I don't think telling his stories had that much to do with vanity. I think he had a deep need to plant a secret he wanted me to find. But I grow angry that he's left me such a mystery, and neither the government, nor the archives, nor the guards, nor the relatives have solved it. At least Dad told me something. I am surprised when Chris sends me a postcard outlining her father's illness, given the family's tendency toward silence and distance. But he did ask me to write about

him, and I have—but without romance. I'm assuming
he'd read my previous books. He knew I would worry
the narrative until it released some kind of truth.

Romance is not about truth.

I abandon the library at the War College's Military History
Institute. I have spent the morning reading various generals' mail, begging letters from fathers asking that their sons
not be put in charge of Negroes or else they'll contact their
congressman, notes to editors to have *Life* subscriptions
forwarded to Tokyo. The facility documents power and
ego, not the actual work of the military as it is recorded at
the National Archives. All I find, amid the boasting, is a
description of an orgy noted by an officer on the first day
of the occupation of Tokyo. I walk out and take a short-
cut over the golf course to return to my room and pack. I
am within sight of the graves of the Indian children again
when I decide to turn back. They remind me of justice.

I just handed the archivist in my citations, I did not
reveal the true nature of my search. I'm afraid I'll get the
same response as I did at NARA—*You nut!*—but here
I'll be escorted off the premises and have all my notes
confiscated. Get a life, I tell myself. They won't be that
interested. After all, sometimes an archivist knows more
than what's listed in the source files.

The man does not flinch. He tells me that 1946 is
a very difficult year for documentation because it's between wars. He's not surprised I've had a lot of trouble
finding material. He suggests I contact various scholars.
I already have the names, but I am very grateful for his
professional attention.

Frank sends me the phone number of his friend Marvin S.,
another ex-guard. Marvin tells me they put two or three
prisoners to death while he was there (1946–1949), maybe

a couple of them from Guam. One of them could've been in for rape. "Black soldiers?" I ask. "I don't remember much," he says. "I was only seventeen. But there I was, sitting up on the tower that night one of the hangings took place. Everybody knew it was happening."

Officially, eighteen people are required to witness a hanging. I find a form marked Secret at the National Archives filled out for an American soldier executed in the Philippines in 1947. It is mixed in with the forms for the executions of Japanese prisoners—I am surprised to discover that we executed twice the number of Japanese (nearly a thousand) than we did Germans—but the form is the same for a Japanese or an American. The following personnel are required:

1 Technician

2 Assistant Technicians

1 Commander of the Special Guard with 1 Assistant

5 Soldiers in the Special Guard

1 Officer of the Day

1 Captain to read the charges

1 Chaplain

1 Major as a witness

2 Guards to escort the prisoner

1 MD or nurse to determine when the prisoner is dead

1 Security Officer

That's a lot of people to keep a secret.

Chaplain Oscar W. Schoech served at the Eighth Army stockade from 1948 on and oversaw the executions of the Japanese war criminals at Sugamo; a Captain Peter Ungavarski was the doctor, according to William M.'s phenomenal memory. Whether or not they served at the stockade in 1946, I will never know. Schoech is the subject of a brief article, "Missionary to War Criminals," but they are both dead, according to newspaper accounts and Ancestry.com, and neither is mentioned in the morning reports, which means that if they were around then, they never reported sick.

The man executed in the Philippines is included in the Pentagon list. I email the Death Penalty Information Center with the date and place of the execution, and they post it. No matter how terrible the crime, a soldier at least should have that.

You hand your son over to the state and expect a truthful accounting of at least his death. "Murdered mysteriously" or "executed with little regard for circumstances" are not the sort of reports that the military likes to provide, but the flak after the execution of one of its own is always going to be bad. Professor Lilly and Alice Kaplan mention that the military in Europe often lied about the executions to the next of kin. Is letting the military not tell the truth about the deaths of its soldiers one of its necessary social lies, imperative for our greater good, like censuring the *New York Times* for telling us the telecom industry was selling information on everyone to the government? Or, even more to the point, keeping secret the fact that friendly fire killed Pat Tillman, the ex–NFL player and soldier? The greater good being that the military needs to attract our sons to enlist in order to protect the country or promote its dominance. It can't afford bad publicity, in Japan or Iraq.

Waiting for my class to convene at Fordham, I catch just a few words from a ROTC lecturer: ". . . in case anyone's hiding under a table or a blanket." One or two black faces and plenty of white ones nod, all nice Catholic kids in full battle drag, sitting ramrod straight, listening to every syllable—so unlike my fiction-writing class. But theirs is a life-or-death subject. Do they realize it's their life or death, or, at the very least, the life or death of someone hiding under a table or blanket?

How did the lecturer's sentence begin, "Let 'er rip"? Or "Use a broom"?

CHAPTER 28

In spring 2007 I make what I hope to be my final visit to the National Archives. I have few leads. I want to copy a page from the court-martial ledgers to remind myself how little information they contain; I want to explore the chaplain records to see if there are reports about executions. After I finish my copying task, the chaplain lead proves to be useless; the box contains only records from after 1946. I return to the wall of indexes for more research.

I read an order from Lieutenant General William Styer, "Commanding General U.S. Armed Forces, Western Pacific," to General MacArthur that states: "Overhead personnel will be reduced as nbr [number] prisoners is reduced however sufficient qualified pers incl technicians for accomplishing executions should be retained. No indication nbr future executions incl War Criminals will diminish." This suggests that "technicians"—executioners—were kept on staff both for the Sugamo war criminals and for the Eighth Army stockade. It is dated April 1946. The letter also estimates 490 of the "unrestorable" prisoners should be returned to the United States, some 300 more than appear on the stockade's rolls. Where are those prisoners?

In the Eighth Army stockade's May report, I find a "Certificate of destruction of classified documents, retained permanently; shows permanent records of Organization destroyed, unauthorized."

All the evidence destroyed in the merry, merry month of May.

More smoke.

A request for a report-of-execution form dated August 7, 1946, from a Captain D. W. Dooley to Second Lieutenant Charles C. Rexroad in the Philippines, suggests that reports of executions in general were rather casual: "If no files are available, it is requested that Lt. Rexroad fill in the form to the best of his ability from memory in cases where he has personal knowledge

"More smoke."

of the executions." "Accomplished" is the reply on August 28 by D. K. Scruby, but no forms in triplicate are attached. Unlike Tojo's executioner, who found the work depressing, Rexroad was "jolly and convivial," according to a June 1948 *Saturday Evening Post* article, "Hanging is His Trade." But he left no papers.

Page 25 of the provost marshal's "History of the Campaigns of the Pacific" talks of twenty-four executions taking place between 1942 and 1947, but its footnote, number fifty-nine out of over a hundred, is the only one that is not included in the back of the manuscript.

An index shows a letter from a Mr. Leon Guess "concerning the number of Negro soldiers executed as a result of courts-martial," dated July 7, 1946, about the time it would take for news of a May execution to get back to the States. But when I search for the letter itself, it's the only one missing from the file, and, according to Ancestry.com, Leon Guess is dead.

I discover that eighteen dishonorable discharges from the Pacific are buried at Clark Field Post in Manila, but none of them appear on my stockade list. "And there are many, many unknowns," says the cemetery's keeper after I call him.

I lie awake that night, realizing that none of the documents I've reviewed about the stockade ever even mention the gallows, either its use or its construction, which, according to my uncle, was so elaborate. The next day I find a letter that explains the highly unusual release of prisoners in Japan—the orders were given by telephone. Were the gallows ordered by telephone too? What else went undocumented that way?

Beginning in the 1960s, the Jews conducted massive oral histories in Germany, unearthing many secrets about the war and our occupation there. Around the same time, many Germans were investigated and prosecuted for lesser war crimes. Eventually nearly every level of involvement with the war there and subsequent occupation gained some transparency. But not so in Japan.

The Japanese have been rewriting their textbooks ever since they signed the peace treaty, particularly with regard to the Rape of Nanking, and their comfort women, in China and Japan. The Americans' suppression of information is not so different.

I decide that the trauma after an execution could not be great enough to make a person kill himself sixty years later. My uncle's conscience would have been exonerated by the group. After all, John T. felt justice was being done when he saw the rope go taut. More likely, the trauma my uncle experienced would have been caused by the death of someone close, at least in proximity, if not emotionally. Either he had befriended the condemned man or he killed someone himself. But an accidental killing like the one described by my father—my uncle's secret—seems also unlikely to cause such a profound haunting. It could be explained as self-defense, as was the violent judo fight with the Japanese cook. Did the eight-hours-on, eight-hours-off routine push him to the edge?

Or did he lie to Dad?

He told Dad the MPs didn't like to chase the escaped prisoners and always forced the cooks to grab the guns and go after them. He said the MPs stayed inside the stockade and waited for the cooks to do their duty.

Dad was a cook—a master sergeant in charge of cooking, he now tells me.

His brother liked to tease.

He was not a liar, Dad tells me on the phone the next morning.

"Why do you want the records of all these horrible criminals?" asks the clerk at the National Personnel Records Center.

I don't believe they're criminals. They're all around twenty years old, from the lowest ranks, it's usually their first offense, the chaos of war or opportunism surrounds them, they've been tempted by the extremely powerful liquor the locals sell. Alice Kaplan's book *The Interpreter* and Professor Lilly's research point out how the illegal moonshine cut with formaldehyde made soldiers crazy in Europe, and my uncle talks about its effects too. Lilly also describes the scant preparation for the hasty trials, where the defendants were so cowed by the process they sometimes didn't even speak up for themselves, about the lack of due process, about missing witnesses, about "the officer senior in rank, [who] often uses his weight and influence to dominate without even a pretense of impartiality; that even when votes are taken in inverse order of rank, the junior officers are perfectly well aware whether they are voting in accordance with his wishes; that the votes are taken orally; that no record of the proceedings is given the person most concerned," according to the House Committee on Military Affairs report.

However, even my uncle says the inmates he guarded were bad. *These were the tough amongst the tough.* Maybe they were. But bad enough to be hanged? Walter Luszki's book, *A Rape of Justice,* includes the letters from the condemned men in New Guinea to their families at

home, and some of them are heartbreaking pleas of innocence. What little I know about the prisoners plays
on the gap between what Wendy Lesser, in *Pictures at an
Execution*, calls the "uncertainties of reality and the dead
certainty of capital punishment." I see the inmates in the
Eighth Army stockade desperately poring over their records, I see the gallows out their windows. I want to know
what happened to these boys.

A chance submission of "death penalty" to Google
brings up a detailed description of the crimes committed by the eighteen men executed at Shepton Mallet in
England. I am appalled: a man who rapes and murders
a pregnant woman, another who rapes a seven-year-old.
My liberal self writhes. I have to remind myself that even
the most grisly accusations are only that, accusations in
that climate of casual convictions.

A few days later I'm reviewing the Wikipedia file on
the death penalty and scan a separate list for those executed by the U.S. Air Force much later than my uncle's
time. The one executed in 1950 seems to fit the execution
William M. remembers happening in 1949. There are also
two executed in Guam that another guard had mentioned
to him as having been executed at the Eighth Army stockade. William reviews the entries and writes back:

> Burns and Dennis were cousins from Philadelphia and Dennis had a
> brother Calvin. All three raped and murdered a Special Service hostess
> on Guam . . . The office I worked in held prisoners personal property
> while they were there, included a copy of their court proceedings.
> When we worked as office CQ at night, with nothing to do but wait for
> incoming prisoners we used to read the proceedings. Those three did
> unspeakable, horrible things to that girl before they killed her . . . the
> [cousins] were hanged at the stockade. The other guy Keller broke into
> the Tachikawa AFB PX. Keller jammed a broken bottle into [the Master

Sgt.'s] throat nearly cutting his head off. His wife and kid were waiting
in the Prison Officers' office while they hanged him in order to claim the
body for stateside shipment. I probably should not comment Burns & his
Dennis cousins were black and the murdered girl was white.

Williams was present for the second execution, and
read the report of the first. He can't imagine why the
places of execution are listed as Yokohama and Guam
when he knows both happened at the stockade. I review
their trials. Maybe it's because they were court-martialed
there, I tell him. Maybe those who were executed at the
Eighth Army stockade in May 1946 (and for the next six
years) were brought there from another U.S. base. I give
up scouring my prisoner lists.

Researchers like to start with Plot E in France, its nice
neat rows of easily identified graves. Who would want
to research the Pacific, with some of the executed taken
home by the next of kin, some buried and then reburied
somewhere else? Besides, I'm trying to research the executions using the vets' recollections rather than the official papers—vets, I might add, who each told me about
the hangings separately.

I read all the recorded courts-martial held in the
Pacific and Europe, and the "Branch Office Cases," the
mysterious bloody red B.O.C. finally spelled out, from
1945 through 1947 via microfilm, no easy "find" button there. I am surprised by how often Judge Advocate
General Thomas H. Green suggests commutation of the
death sentence. But the House Committee on Military
Affairs report says that he could suggest commutation all
he wanted, but that the commanding general "not infrequently rejects or ignores it."

The charges are terrible: getting a gun and waiting for
the wife to return to the house, strangling three women,

and, most commonly, shooting a fellow soldier. From these records, it seems that only two executions were carried out during those years in the Pacific. *It seems* because as always with these government forms, sometimes there's a date of execution and sometimes not. Needless to say, there's no location. Sometimes the same court-martial is entered twice. The bottom line is that these records say no one in Japan was executed for rape in 1946.

I guess those five vets didn't see anything.

In July 2007 I find "Relations Between Allied Forces and the Population of Japan," a historiography posted on the internet a month earlier by its author, Bertrand M. Roehner, a scholar in France. He has examined the Allied-occupation archives in Australia, Britain, and New Zealand and scoured the Japanese and American newspapers in his research. Few American archives were available. His findings contradict many historians' view of Japan's "benevolent cooperation," especially that of the Pulitzer Prize–winning John Dower, whose most famous statement about the postwar period I've already quoted: "There was not a single incident of terrorism against the U.S. forces there after World War II."

Immediately after the peace treaty was signed, the Japanese twice shot down aerial photographers, killing one. Between 1945 and 1960 they dropped leaflets, de-railed trains, engaged in wire cutting, blocked roads with boulders, plotted to assassinate MacArthur at least twice, and repeatedly stoned, assaulted, and shot at servicemen. They held many demonstrations sometimes with up to a quarter million people in attendance. I am especially struck by the number of cases of arson—sixty-seven in the first three months of 1947 alone, fires that destroyed over $1 million worth of U.S. property in those three months and resulted in the deaths of six servicemen. These many accidents never attributed as sabotage to the Japanese remind Roehner of the frequent "mechanical failures" of the helicopters in Iraq in the early stages of the war, and how 81 percent of the fatalities of the occupation troops at that time were blamed on accidents. I wonder about the circumstances behind the deaths of five soldiers all on the same day, November 22, 1945, at Misawa Naval Air Base. All I found was a list of personal effects, no report.

Sometimes the Allied soldiers retaliated or even instigated the violence. I better understand my uncle's cigarette scam—which Roehner details—and my uncle having been found with "a couple extra watches, some extra, extra yen" after I read that General Eichelberger twice had to admonish the troops for their behavior, citing looting, rape, and robbery. General Eisenhower ordered a report on troop behavior in 1946 in both Japan and the Philippines. (The National Archives has the report's cover sheet, but no report can be found.) Roehner cites the high incidence of traffic accidents, something I too had noticed—963 in Tokyo alone during April 1946—noting that the Allied forces were nearly the only ones with cars and that perhaps soldiers were deliberately running down civilians. He quotes a B. Browley, a New Zealand soldier: "To my shock there were quite a number of Kiwis who did mean harm. I was horrified on the several occasions where, otherwise reasonable chaps, would not only deliberately accelerate their trucks to give the Japs a fright, but actually boast about it later. One sergeant killed two Japanese announcing, 'I'm going to get me a gook.' Well, he got two and the matter was hushed up." The monthly average of Japanese killed in traffic accidents by military vehicles is forty-five. As for rapes, Roehner doesn't involve himself in those numbers because, he reasons, rape is so underreported in peacetime as well as wartime, but he does mention that even as late as April 1952 the *New York Times* reported that Japan's most prominent female leader begged General Ridgway's daughter to isolate the immoral U.S. troops. The death toll on the Japanese side can be estimated from the 4,339 claims paid by the Japanese government for its citizens who died as a result of the actions of the occupation, no doubt far fewer than the actual count, according to Roehner.

This is a surprise to me, emails William M., the vet who has provided such detailed information about the Eighth Army stockade.

How could the servicemen realize how dangerous the occupation was? MacArthur censored newspapers, radio, movies old and new, lantern slides, theatrical scripts and performances, Kabuki, Bunraku, plays, music, songs, postage stamps and currency, books, magazines and journals, speeches, teaching courses, mail, phone, and the telegraph. "Even the Allied military reports were subject to self-censorship," writes Roehner. MacArthur also forbade any mention of even the existence of censorship in the press, and exiled or fired *Stars and Stripes* editors as well as the *Times, Saturday Evening Post,* and *Christian Science Monitor* correspondents who didn't obey. Meanwhile the *Stars and Stripes* ran headlines like "Hokkaido Trouble Greatly Exaggerated."

Every historian agrees that MacArthur's policy of silence and censorship allowed the occupation to succeed. With both sides blood soaked and furious, it was truly a miracle that peace held and continued. But were secret executions part of the price? It's important for us to know now the victors' cost of "creating peace."

But we do not even know how many U.S. soldiers died during the occupation. Because of the lack of access to records, we can only extrapolate: the British in the Allied forces in Japan showed a fatality rate of 4.5 soldiers a month per 10,000 troops, the same fatality rate of American forces in Iraq monthly between 2003 and 2005.

"The so-called Military Government courts or Military Commissions could impose death sentences," but this information is not available, writes Roehner. Roehner tells me there are many more courts-martial than I have reviewed. I had been wondering why I'd only seen at most thirty courts-martial for rape between 1945 and 1947, when John Dower reported 330 a month after MacArthur's crackdown on prostitution in 1946.

Even in 1946 the House Committee on Military Affairs found it hard to get information: "The most tragic [of excessive sentences], of course, are the death sentences not commuted, about which it is so difficult to obtain information. Many of these have been for rape, especially abroad."

On May 25, 1946, the *Christian Science Monitor* ran a cartoon about military justice captioned "Time to Add a Few Pages?" A female justice holds a sheaf of paper labeled Effective Protection of Individual Rights over a book entitled Military Court System. Armies can make mistakes, innocent soldiers can be killed or, at the very least, their

"Time to Add a Few Pages?"

paperwork lost. But the only time I found anyone's execution papers, they were filed with the Japanese and marked Secret. These records should be transparent and easy to discover and above all truthful. Suspicion rears its ugly head if they are not. None of this finding a list stuffed behind a file cabinet in the Pentagon. There's the stench of lynching, with so many black soldiers unaccounted for, with the convenient execution of a black man for rape at a time when MacArthur needed an example.

Now I'm wondering if there were executed soldiers who didn't get a spot in Plot E.

CHAPTER 30

This time the National Archives summons me. My Freedom of Information Act requests are ready to be viewed. All I have to do is travel to D.C. and request a box named Dummy.

Two days later I am grinning with anticipation, asking for the Dummy box. But no one can find it. Someone comes out from the back and someone is called. I wait an hour. In the interim, I talk to another researcher, an old hand, who rolls his eyes when I tell him I have to wait. "Sounds like they're going through it," he says.

Finally the Dummy box appears. Two documents lie inside it, a letter about a major who was taking kickbacks from Japanese construction firms, and a report about the stockade in 1950.

I return the box. I muster my notes. My friend the researcher says I should make copies of what they've produced. I ask for the box back and copy the contents. Disgusted all over again, I return it. Then, fuming, I settle down to wait for new material I've just ordered. Nothing appears. For hours. Finally I am told there are new rules. The second time I took out the Dummy box, I didn't sign it back in. They need a signature; this policy started the week before. It doesn't matter that I hadn't been offered the form. I am forever ineligible to see anything else because I still have something out. The woman behind the desk shrugs. Her supervisor, the (now retired) expert in the occupation, is out to lunch. Ten minutes later, he is at a meeting.

The Dummy box.

History is composed of lies, official and personal. So many of the prisoners and guards alike lied about their ages to get into the army. Both birth certificates and enlistment papers sit at Ancestry.com's site, waiting for someone to put the two together.

The present is a forest of questions. Such harmless lies show only the boys' enthusiasm to serve.

I've stumbled on something bigger, investigating my uncle's story. Roehner emails me about "omertà." A Mafia term, the French use it to mean "any information which is well known by a few people yet not openly recognized." If my uncle's story smokes in the aftermath of Abu Ghraib, and the "burners," those precursors to shredders, have escaped, then history must read that smoke.

The Uniform Code of Military Justice (UCMJ) was passed in 1950, partly as a result of the 1946 House Committee on Military Affairs, but even more because of the shocking revelation that one in eight soldiers in World War II was court-martialed, some two million cases. Commanders still have great leeway. "In a capital trial in which individual rights are balanced with the prerogative of command, the risks posed to due process are greater than in the earlier justice system," says a lawyer whose client was on death row in 1999.

In May 2007, military contractors finally found themselves under UCMJ, under the same rules as the military, but only during a declared war.

. . .

I am neither the guilt-ridden, nearly dead MP uncle dictating his memoirs nor the puzzled archivist, nor one of the grieving members of the family of the mysteriously lost soldiers. But I complain. You condone what goes on if you don't complain. My taxes have already paid for what goes on, and, inasmuch as they pay for the slaughter and torture of the innocents in Iraq, I've also paid for whatever went on in that stockade. At least my forebears paid. We also paid for sixty years with the struggles of desegregation and de facto separation. Now we pay differently for the haunting of the country's veterans.

With post-traumatic stress you relive the experience, you actually see everything all over again. The wheat fields and the big equipment and the chocolate bar on your dash don't appear as objects in your brain; instead you actually see whatever that terrible sight is that you can't forget. Like staring too long at a bright light, you see the bright light everywhere.

As a family, we have no talent for acting, we have no talent for speaking. Miming, maybe. Charades at every family party allows each relative to come forward and be recognized, for ill or for good. At Dad's eighty-third birthday party I mime *Madame Butterfly,* a challenge because opera knowledge is not part of the family skill set or was forgotten after Sarah Bernhardt made her last trip west. I go for the whole concept: I am a butterfly, wiggling in my chrysalis, bursting forth. They guess *Hair,* the musical. I am the geisha with a sad face. They guess Marcel Marceau. I am on a boat, waving and saluting, and it's obvious—*The Mikado.*

Dad is the one who guesses it, three seconds before the kitchen timer goes off.

My uncle's son Tom says he's seen *Madame Butterfly,*

only the one where she's a he. He's our Mensa member; he's memorized the contents of the potato chips, all forty-three ingredients, he's a charming redneck of the worst sort, the wealthy sort. He once mentioned to me long ago that his father had a Jap boy older than he was. I thought it was just a self-important story told to make him seem exotic, with a Japanese half brother—*Go on*— or else some oblique way to explain why he never graduated from college.

He never imagines it's a girl. Or no one at all, a baby that starved.

Ten months into the occupation, General MacArthur had a Japanese radio announcer fired for referring to the birth of a GI baby as "the first occupation present." He felt information like that would provide "anti-American propaganda for the jingoes and the Communists," according to Peter Kalischer's article "Madame Butterfly's Children," which ran in *Collier's* in 1952. Between five thousand and fifteen thousand babies were born as a result of the occupation. Kalischer ends the piece with a quote from Lieutenant Colonel John J. Power, chaplain for a naval battery that donated a percentage of their pay to support a mixed-race orphanage: "From what I've seen of what these kids have to contend with, they may develop into the greatest class of featherweight fighters in the world."

My uncle's baby had a fighter's genes. But he was forgotten by his father, his family, all of us, the whole country, dismissed as the wages of war. Only three of the nine hundred graves of occupation babies buried at Negishi Foreign Cemetery in Yokohama are marked.

Suicide confers a kind of immortality on the victim, of life arrested, a photo forever fixed, Superman with his cape unfurled behind him, his fists clenched. The suicide is here and then gone, he doesn't linger with illness and get weak and fade away. Unlike the accident victim, he says good-bye, he knows. He never has to answer for his act.

"I was arguing with myself. Then there were two separate selves, and one of them finally shot the other so that I shot myself," said a veteran of the Vietnam War, dreaming of being both the executioner and the victim, in Robert Jay Lifton's book *Home from the War.*

"He had a great run," writes Chris, who loved him so much.

My uncle will never pay me for the transcription, Chris will never return my calls, Dad will find something not quite right in the book—but I wrestle with the story anyway. I'm just sorry that I can't produce any bodies other than my uncle's. I absolutely reject the suggestion that he was deranged when he made the tapes. I could continue circling footnotes for years, becoming more obsessed, harassing archivists and historians and librarians from here to Tokyo, to Korea even, where the Eighth Army stockade's history is said to reside, although no one there will answer my phone calls, emails, or letters. But I won't stand for my uncle's ghost teasing me, hovering over my shoulder where I'm hunched over some huge pile of documents at the National Archives. I declare the job finished.

"You kept him alive," repeats my cousin, "with that taping."

Armies deal in death. They have to threaten other nations, to threaten their own soldiers into compliance.

. . .

If GIs were indeed hanged at the stockade, it suggests that every war or occupation creates its monsters, terrible incidents that happen in the ambience of killing, senseless— military killing, the senseless—as in *no-feeling*—killing. Right or wrong, we need to know about such incidents. We need to wake up and face the nightmare, the dangling body, because we pay for the terror and torture with the minds of our soldiers. It's a symptom of the degeneration of a society when such behavior is hidden. The society begins to stink, no matter what. Or is this just what we think, or hope—how many times do the cover-ups work and no one ever knows? The word *mystery* means "to close the eyes or mouth." My uncle opened his, and then opened it wider for the shotgun.

My Superman.

WORKS CITED

CHAPTER 1

the Rush Limbaugh: Media Matters for America: Rush Limbaugh Transcripts. 2004. Media Matters for America. May 4, 2004. 15 Oct 2007. <http://mediamatters.org/items/200405130002>

Abu Ghraib's Infant Formula Plant: "Was It a Baby Milk Factory?" *Washington Post.* 1998. The Washington Post Company. 15 Oct 2007. <http://www.washington post.com/wp-srv/inatl/longterm/fogofwar/vignettes/v4.htm>

CHAPTER 2

"Racial agitation": MacGregor, Jr., Morris J. "Segregation's Consequences." *Defense Studies Series: Integration of the Armed Forces 1940–1965.* 1979. 2 May 2001. 15 Oct 2007. <www.army.mil/CMH/books/integration/IAF-08.htm>

CHAPTER 3

"They keep trying to get me . . .": Sabin, Burritt. "They Came, They Saw, They Democratized." *Japan Times* 28 April 2002. Also Manchester, William. *American Caesar: Douglas MacArthur 1880–1965.* Boston: Little, Brown, 1978. 468–469.

Roehner, Bertrand M. *Relations Between Allied Forces and The Population of Japan 15 August 1945–31 December 1960*. Paris: University of Paris, 2007. 26.

an MP named Joseph Darby: "Joe Darby." *Wikipedia*. Oct 2007. 20 Sep 2007. <http://en.wikipedia.org/wiki/Joe_Darby>

CHAPTER 4

"set the conditions": "Iraq: Applying Counter-Terrorism Tactics during a Military Occupation." *Human Rights Watch*. June 2004. <http://hrw.org/reports/2004/usa0604/5.htm>

"enhanced interrogation techniques": Ross, Brian and Richard Esposito, "CIA's Harsh Interrogation Techniques Described." *ABC News*. 18 Nov 2005. Transcript. 19 Oct 2007. <http://abcnews.go.com/Blotter/Investigation/story?id=1322866>

"poorest in the entire country": Frank, Thomas. "What's the Matter with Kansas? How Conservatives Won the Heart of America." *Trampled Dreams: The Neglected Economy of the Rural Great Plains*. Comp. Patricia Funk and John Bailey. Walthill: Center for Rural Affairs, 2000. 6.

CHAPTER 5

In his essay: On the Natural History of Destruction: W.G. Sebald. "The Remorse of the Heart." New York: Penguin, 2004. 169–192.

The famed biographer Janet Malcolm: Malcolm, Janet. *The Silent Woman*. New York: Vintage Books, 1995. 154–155.

CHAPTER 6

"Killing is what war is all about...": Grossman, Lt. Col. David. *On Killing: The Psychological Cost of Learning to Kill in War and Society.* Boston: Back Bay Books, 1996. 93.

"The dead soldier takes his misery with him...": Grossman, Lt. Col. David. 93.

"Many lawyers and others...": United States. House of Representatives Committee on Military Affairs. *Investigations of the National War Effort, Report of the Committee of Military Affairs, House of Representatives, 79th Congress, Second Session, Pursuant to H. Res. 20: A Resolution Authorizing the Committee on Military Affairs to Study the Progress of the National War Effort, June 1946.* GPO, 1946. 12.

Twenty out of twenty-one reported executions: "List of Individuals Executed by the United States Military." *Wikipedia.* 2003. 22 Sep 2007. <http://users.bestweb.net/~rg/execution/WWII%20MILITARY%20EXECUTIONS%20PACIFIC.htm>

CHAPTER 7

Ten acres in total: Mahar, William. "Re: 8th Army Stockade statistics." Email to author. 17 Aug 2007 and 17 Oct 2007.

largest stockade in all of Asia: Mamoru, Makino, dir. *The Relief Disappearing in the Light—Nakano Prison.* Self-distributed. 1983.

Chuck Mayne: Mayne, Chuck. Telephone interview with author. 20 July 2006.

Abu Ghraib is the contemporary version: "Abu Ghraib." *Wikipedia.* Oct 2003. 20 Sep 2006. <http://en.wikipedia .org/wiki/Abu_Ghraib_prison>

"The occupation of Japan had great moral and legal . . . There was not a single incidence of terrorism . . .": Wallis, David. "Questions for John W. Dower: Occupation Preoccupation." *The New York Times.* 30 Mar 2003. 9.

"20 yen—a buck . . ." Costello, John. *Love, Sex, and War: Changing Values 1939–1945.* London: William Collins, 1985. 346–347. *Heretical.* 15 Oct 2007. <http:// www.heretical.com/costello/16yield.html>

CHAPTER 8

"Nowhere in these postwar documents . . .": Kaplan, Alice. *The Interpreter.* New York: Free Press/Simon and Schuster, 2005. 156.

"They shot some of those guys . . .": Terkel, Studs. *The Good War.* New York: New Press, 2004. 390.

equal number of blacks and whites: "Author Survey." Survey. *Ancestry.com.* 20 July 2006. <http://www.ancestry .com/>

M., Chan, 1. Interview with author. 4 July 2006.

B., Ben, 2. Interview with author. 4 July 2006.

B., Marvin, 3. Interview with author. 4 July 2006.

". . . 38% decline in black recruiting . . .": Baldor, Lolita C. "Number of Blacks Joining Military Down." *Washington Post, AP.* 24 June 2007.

similar hesitation killing Japanese: Buckley, Gail. *American Patriots: The Story of Blacks in the Military from the Revolution to Desert Storm.* New York: Random House, 2001. 272.

"Instead of widespread raping, looting...": United States. U.S. Army. *Soldiers Guide to Japan.* GPO, 1946. 4.

CHAPTER 9

"The past is never dead.": Padgett, John B. *"Requiem for a Nun:* Resources." *William Faulkner on the Web.* 17 Aug 2006. Ed. John B. Padgett. U of Mississippi. 16 Oct 2007. <http://www.mcsr.olemiss.edu/~egjbp/faulkner/r_n_rfan.html>.

'sit-down cells,' the so-called Japanese boxes: United States. U.S. Department of the Army. *Prisoners, General Provisions: Personnel 1048, Army Regulations No. 600–375.* GPO, 1948. 32.

"... is virtually inseparable from military discipline...": Lurie, Jonathan. *Military Justice in America.* Lawrence: University Press of Kansas, 2001. 47.

"I've heard about 30,000 troops...": Lilly, Robert. "Re: "Japanese War Trial Records." Email to author. 17 Aug 2005.

CHAPTER 11

"The law which a condemned man..." Kafka, Franz. "In the Penal Colony." Johnstonia. Trans. Ian Johnston. 19 Feb 2007. 15 Oct 2007. <http://www.mala.bc.ca/~johnstoi/kafka/inthepenalcolony.htm>

Lt. Michael Drayton: "Chaos and Violence at Abu Ghraib." *BBC News.* May 2004. 15 Oct 2007. <http://news.bbc.co.uk/1/hi/world/americas/3690097.stm.>

CHAPTER 12

called variously soldier's heart: Hyams K.C., S. Wignall and R. Roswell. "War Syndromes and their Evaluations: From the US Civil War to the Persian Gulf War." *Annals of Internal Medicine* 125 (1996) 398–405. For the Odysseus diagnosis, I am indebted to Shay, Jonathan. *Odysseus in America: Combat Stress and the Trials of Homecoming.* New York: Scribner, 2002.

CHAPTER 13

"Let me point out that the prisoners . . .": Pearl, Jack. *Stockade.* New York: Trident Press, 1965. 55.

Officially, there were no escapes: "Return of General Prisoners" A1–149; 8th Army Stockade 1946; General Correspondence, 1946–1951; Provost Marshal Section, Far East Command, Department of Defense, Record Group 554; National Archives at College Park, College Park, MD.

Shock treatment is the preferred: Delmaestro, Susan. Telephone interview. 5 Oct 2005.

CHAPTER 14

I did read that MacArthur had the chaplains: Herbison, Chico, and Schultz, Ed. *Quiet Passages: Study Guide to The Japanese-American War Bride Experience.* Law-

rence: The Center for East Asian Studies, University of
Kansas, 1990. 4.

Defense Secretary Rumsfeld: United States. Department
of Defense. *Operational Update Briefing.* By Defense
Secretary Donald Rumsfeld. Transcript. 4 May 2004.
15 Oct 2007. <http://www.defenselink.mil/transcripts/
transcript.aspx?transcriptid=2973>

*"Bring in the guilty bastard . . . Give the man a fair
trial . . .":* Lilly, Robert J. "Dirty Details: Executing U.S.
Soldiers During World War II." Diss. Northern Kentucky
University, 1995. 6.

Details about hanging: Lilly, Robert J. 10.

". . . Sadaam's half-brother . . .": Tarabay, Jamie. "All
Things Considered." *National Public Radio.* 15 Jan
2007. Transcript. 15 Jan 2007. <http://www.npr.org/
templates/story/story.php?storyId=6861053>

". . . 'acquittals at 4 percent' and 'their pay stops . . .'":
United States. House of Representatives Committee on
Military Affairs. 6.

The prison's PR department: Lifton, Robert Jay and
Greg Mitchell. *Who Owns Death: Capital Punishment,
the American Conscience, and the End of Executions.*
New York: Harper Perennial, 2002. 120.

*1946 was the year a black veteran had his eyes gouged
out":* Uscupstate.com: *Resonant Ripples in a Global
Pond: The Blinding of Isaac Woodard.* 15 Oct 2007.
<http://faculty.uscupstate.edu/amyers/woodard.html>

"In 1946 Paul Robeson . . .": Spartacus.schoolnet.co
.uk: *Paul Robeson.* <http://www.spartacus.schoolnet
.co.uk/USArobeson.htm>

It was also in 1946 that Lieutenant General Eichel-berger: Eichelberger, Lt. General. Letter to Command-ing Officer, Eighth Army Stockade. 20 Sep 1946. General Correspondence Files ca. 1947; Adjutant General Sec-tion, IX Corps; Far East Command, Department of De-fense; Record Group 338; National Archives at College Park, MD.

CHAPTER 15

A white boy from Jersey: United States. Military News-paper. Pacific *Stars and Stripes.* Tokyo, Japan. 28 Mar 1946.

The court received: United States. Office of the JAG. *Holdings, Opinions, and Reviews: v.1–81 + 2 index volumes.* GPO, 1924–1949 and 1944–1949.

A Time magazine article: "Mercy." 20 May 1946. Also Letter to the Editor. 10 June 1946. *Time Magazine.*

Hicswa's mother complained: Cowee, John. Telephone interview. 14 Apr 2007.

CHAPTER 16

940 people committed suicide in 1935: Marcus, Eric. *Why Suicide?* New York: HarperOne, 1996. 46.

CHAPTER 17

135 American soldiers since 1916: "Closing Ranks on Executions, Military Nears First Death Penalty Since JFK; Policy Assailed." National Law Journal. 5 Apr 1999. A1.

The military executed 141: United States. House of Representatives Committee on Military Affairs. 6.

160 men executed between 1942 and 1962: United States. *Statistical Abstracts of the United States: No. 375.* GPO, 2000. 25.

A list of 154 executed men: "Executions in the Military." Chart. *Death Penalty Information Center.* 17 Sep 2007. <http://www.deathpenaltyinfo.org/article.php?scid=32&did=988>

In December 2003, a document was discovered at the Pentagon that listed the executions under United States military jurisdiction from 1945 through 1961.": Lilly, J. Robert. "Death Penalty Cases in World War II Military Courts: Lessons Learned from North Africa and Italy." ts. 41st Annual Meeting of the Academy of Criminal Justice Sciences. Las Vegas, Nevada. 10–13 Mar 2004. 34.

CHAPTER 18

"The prisoners thought that we were doctors...": Easton, Thomas. "A Quiet Honesty Records a World War II Atrocity." *Tokyo Bureau of The Baltimore Sun.* 28 May 1995.

skulls and thigh bones of 101 people: McGill, Peter, and Roy K. Akagawa. "Consumed by the Devil's Gluttony." *Asahi Evening News.* 20 Oct 1997.

just tossed out the bodies: Yamaguchi, Mari. "Quiet Tokyo Neighborhood May Be Sitting On Gruesome Secret." *Japan Times.* 20 Sep 2006. 4 Jun 2006. <http://findarticles.com/p/articles/mi_qn4155/is_20060918/ai_n16733825>

In September 2006: Yamaguchi, Mari.

unprosecuted in exchanged for their data: Rea, David C., dir. *Unit 731—Did the Emperor Know?* Channel 4. 27 Apr 1991.

Dr. Masaji Kitano, the major general: McGill, Peter, and Roy K. Akagawa.

Although a guard writes to me: M., William. Email to author. Re: 8th Army. 22 Jan 2006.

some 267 bodies found in the streets of Tokyo in April 1946: Herbison, Chico, and Schultz, Ed. 4.

CHAPTER 19

where the MPs slept: M., William. Email to author. "Re: 10 times." 18 May 2007.

the prison video: Mamoru, Makino, dir.

Eastern State Penitentiary: EasternState.org.: Eastern State Penitentiary. 15 Oct 2007. <http://www.eastern state.org/history>

CHAPTER 20

World War II vets dying at the rate of 1,500 a day: Brunnstrom, David. "Battlefield Return Brings Closure for WW2 Vets." *Reuters.* 11 May 2007. 16 Oct 2007. <http://www.reuters.com/article/latestCrisis/idUSL11425091>

Korean War vet A.G. Corey: Corey, A.G. Telephone interview. 10 July 2005.

"Oh, they hung a lot of people . . .": McMillen, Joanne. "Interview with Billy Fyffe." Eastern Oklahoma History

Collection, Midwest City Rotary Club. 24 June 2004. <http://www.rose.edu/EOCRHC/MWCRotary.htm>

"We thought we had managed all right . . .": Holmes, Richard. *Acts of War: The Behavior of Men in Battle.* Florence: Free Press, 1989. 399.

Susan Delmaestro . . .": Delmaestro, Susan. Telephone interview. 5 Oct 2005.

"The more serious of these wartime parallels . . .": Uhl, Michael. "Vietnam's Shadow over Abu Ghraib." *Anti-War.* 31 July 2004. 15 Oct 2007. <http://www.antiwar.com/orig/uhl.php?articleid=3219>

I read Greg Hartley's: Hartley, Greg and Maryann Karinch. *How to Spot a Liar: Why People Don't Tell the Truth and How You Can Catch Them.* Franklin Lakes: Career Press, 2005.

"Seeing a man . . .": S., Frank. Letter to the author. 1 Feb 2006 and 8 June 2006.

P., Nick. Telephone interview. 10 Nov 2005.

An Australian researcher: Hoare, Tony. "Veterans, PSTD, Depression and Dementia." Powerpoint. 5th Biennial International Conference. Australian Government Department of Veterans' Affairs, 2004. Slide 9.

"Unless there's strict leadership . . .": Zimbardo, Philip. Interview. *PBS.* 11 May 2004. Transcript. 16 Oct 2007. <http://www.pbs.org/newshour/bb/middle_east/jan-june 04/prisoners_5-11.html>

"Move over, God, it's Mac.": Luszki, Walter. *A Rape of Justice.* Toronto: Madison Press Books, 1991.

Manchester, William. 360.

"We hanged twenty-two yanks in one morning.": Lilly, J. Robert. "Death Penalty Cases in World War II Military Courts: Lessons Learned from North Africa and Italy." 41st Annual Meeting of the Academy of Criminal Justice Sciences. Las Vegas, Nevada. 10–13 Mar 2004. 44.

CHAPTER 21

Private Slovik's execution: Huie, William Bradford. *The Execution of Private Slovik.* 1954. Chicago: Westholme Publishing, 2004.

"The U.S. Army Air Corps . . ." Grossman, Lt. Col. David. 30.

"only 15 to 20 percent": Grossman, Lt. Col. David. 4.

"the simple and demonstrable fact . . .": Grossman, Lt. Col. David. 4.

"It is interesting to note that the subject . . .": Tanaka, Yuki. 123.

In his memoir": Clifton, Allen. *Time of Fallen Blossoms.* New York: Knopf, 1951.

CHAPTER 22

Then I find, deep within: Inspection of 483rd MP E.G. Company; 25 January 1946; Office of the Provost Marshal; Headquarters, 8th Army, Record Group 331; National Archives at College Park, College Park, MD.

Camp McCoy: I was so excited by this discovery I didn't get the citation!

Months later I discover: Photograph SC416030 32/244; *"James E. Baumer 483rd in NM 1952 near Ft. Hood TX in April during Exercise Longhorn in a secret area for project 13766"*; 1952; Records of the Office of the Chief Signal Officer, 1860–1982. Record Group 111; National Archives at College Park, College Park, MD.

They become Headquarters and Headquarters: Special Orders No. 110, 483rd MP E.G. Morning Reports, 27 April 1946; Office of Commander. National Archives and Records Administration. Courtesy of National Personnel Records Center, St. Louis, Missouri.

the court-martial ledger: General Court Martial Offense Ledger Sheets, Vol. 23–28; Records of the Adjutant General's Office; Judge Advocate General, 1946; Record Group 153; National Archives at College Park, College Park, MD.

B.O.C.: Baker, Rich. "Re: Major Knight." Email to the author. 21 Sep 2006.

The librarian I call: Lavering, Dan. Telephone interview. 22 Mar 2006.

A burner: Zobel, James. Telephone interview. 31 Mar 2006.

"Sentences of death . . .": United States. House of Representatives Committee on Military Affairs. 13.

CHAPTER 23

stonewalling: In all fairness, the NARA archivists were under siege during many of my visits, having had their budget slashed and their services to the public severely curtailed—another way government documents are kept secret.

Return of General Prisoners: "Return of General Prisoners" A1–149; 8th Army Stockade 1946; General Correspondence, 1946–1951; Provost Marshal Section, Far East Command, Department of Defense, Record Group 554; National Archives at College Park, College Park, MD.

April report: Monthly Occupation Historical Reports; File 108-DE (4)-.0.2; Central Records Depot; March 1946–June 1946. Record Group 407; National Archives at College Park, College Park, MD.

720 MP unit: Historical Report for Month of September; 720th MP Battalion Historical Report: 4 October 1946; S-3 Section APO 201; Record Group 331; National Archives at College Park, College Park, MD.

prisoners were shipped to Camp McQuaide: Evacuation of General Prisoners. File 200.3–250.1. Provost Marshal General Correspondence 1946–47. Records of General Headquarters, Far East Command, Supreme Commander Allied Powers, and United Nations Command, 1945–1957; Record Group 554; National Archives at College Park, College Park, MD.

Seventh-Day Adventists bought: Monterey Bay Academy: Beginnings. Ed. Monterey Bay Academy. 15 Oct 2007. <http://www.montereybayacademy.org/history/history.html>

Burial—Court Martialed Military Personnel: Burial—Court Martialed Military Personnel; A1 2110-C; 293. GRSPac (Dishonorable Status); Office of the Quartermaster General; Record Group 92; National Archives at College Park, College Park, MD.

discharged in Japan: Chisholm's Discharge Papers. National Archives and Records Administration. Courtesy of National Personnel Records Center, St. Louis, Missouri.

The West Point major: Knight, Major Peter. Telephone interview. 12 Mar 2006 and M., Maha, Re: 8th Army. Email to author. 17 Feb 2006.

seven days in isolation: Re: Solitary Confinement. Letter to Commanding General from James A. Rhodes, Prison Officer 4 Sep 1946. Provost Marshal, Eighth Army. Record Group 338; National Archives at College Park, College Park, MD.

are listed to sail: United States. Request for Travel Orders, 19 Sept 1946; File 220.68 to 250.414; Records of US Army Operations, Tactical and Support, 8th Army; AG Section; U.S. Army; Record Group 338; National Archives at College Park, College Park, MD.

"I have kept asking myself . . .": Sebald, W. G. "An Attempt at Restitution." *The New Yorker.* 20 Dec 2004.

file labeled Executions: Report of Executions; Entry 156 (A1); 7 Aug 1946. Records of Far East Command SCAP and UN Command 1945–57; Provost Marshal Section; Record Group 554; National Archives at College Park, College Park, MD.

I've seen the file where MacArthur asks: General MacArthur memo to Commanding General, Eighth Army; Commanding General, Pacific Air Command; Commanding General, U.S. Army Forces, Western Pacific; Commanding General XXIV Corps; Commanding General, U.S. Army Forces, Middle Pacific. 27 Apr 1946. Records of Adjutant General's Office 1940–1948; Record

Group 407; National Archives at College Park, College Park, MD.

But no, says his archivist: Zobel, James. "Re: May." Email to author. 21 June 2007.

The Harry S. Truman Library: Sowell, Randy. "Re: Pardons." Email to author. 31 Aug 2007.

President Lincoln granted a record: Ruckman, Jr., P.S. and David Kincaid. "Inside Lincoln's Clemency Decision Making." Forthcoming, *Presidential Studies Quarterly.* 2 July 2007. <http://ednet.rvc.cc.il.us/~PeterR/Papers/paper4.htm>

Documents sent to me: National Archives and Records Administration. Courtesy of National Personnel Records Center, St. Louis, Missouri. 44 out of 50 requests filled.

The interviewer of the chief jailor: Mayne, Chuck. Interview. *World War II: Through the Eyes of Cape Fear.* 17 Oct 2001. 16 Oct 2007. <http://capefearww2.uncwil.edu/voices/092bio.html>

He emails back: M., William. "Re: 8th Army." Email to author. 22 Jan 2006.

64,846 replacements: United States. U.S. Army Printing Plant. *A Short History of the 8th Army in Japan: 30 August 1945–1 May 1946.* GPO, 1946. 1.

suspicious: P., Daryl. Telephone interview. 8 July 2006.

four MPs from the Northwest: Chan M., Ben. B., Eugene R., Martin B., 4 July 2006. Telephone interview; and Theodore M. with Otis H. Telephone interview. 6 July 2006.

I'm sure he's dying: D., Irv. Telephone interview. 7 June 2006.

"All autobiographical memory...": Passerini, Luisa. Epigraph. *Remembering: Writing Oral History.* Ed. Anna Green and Megan Hutching. Auckland: Auckland University Press, 2004.

CHAPTER 24

"The sentry is almost certain...": Hankoff, L.D.. "Interaction Patterns Among Military Prison Personnel." *The Military Prison: Theory Research and Practice.* Ed. Brodsky, Stanley, and Eggleston, Norman, American Sociological Association. Illinois: Southern Illinois Press, 1970. 58.

Two or three of the prisoners die in Korea: Bussey, Lt. Col. Charles M. *Firefight at Yechon: Courage and Racism in the Korean War.* Lincoln: University of Nebraska Press, 2002. 81.

"What about all those prisoners...": Pearl, Jack. *Stockade.* New York: Trident Press, 1965. 300–301.

He quotes Donald Cabana: Lifton, Robert Jay and Greg Mitchell. *Who Owns Death: Capital Punishment, the American Conscience, and the End of Executions.* New York: Harper Perennial, 2002. 106.

After Ivan Turgenev: Lifton, Robert Jay and Greg Mitchell. 170–171.

CHAPTER 25

Old men with guns: "Males and Firearms Violence" in *Who Dies?–A Look at Firearms Death and Injury in America, rev. ed.* GPO: Violence Policy Center, 1999.

CHAPTER 26

Despite the average boy seeing sixteen thousand TV murders": Walsh, D., LS Goldman, and RL Brown. "Physician Guide to Media Violence." *American Medical Association.* 1996.

"A virgin observer . . .": Grossman, Lt. Col. David. 2.

We have six times more prisoners: Cassel, Elaine and Douglas A. Bernstein. *Criminal Behavior.* 2nd ed. New Jersey: Laurence Erlbaum Associates, 2007. 260.

"That's what we were there for . . .": M., Vincent, Jack W., Leroy S., and John J. Telephone interviews. 13 Apr 2007.

one in four GIs had come down with VD.: Tanaka, Yuki. 161.

forced to completely reverse his stance: Tanaka, Yuki. 162.

"the number of rapes . . .": Dower, John. 579, fn 16.

Two incidents of mass rape: Tanaka, Yuki. 163–164.

I find Burnam W. Kimmel: United States. *Extract-Special Orders No. 110" 483rd Morning Report.* ts 27 April 1946. National Archives and Records Administration. Courtesy of National Personnel Records Center. St. Louis, Missouri.

S., Richard. Telephone interview. 13 Apr 2007.

C., John. Telephone interview. 14 Apr 2007.

S., Larry. Telephone interview. 13 Apr 2007.

H., Roger. Telephone interview. 14 Apr 2007.

Oral historian Luisa Passerini: Passerini, Luisa. "Women's Personal Narratives: Myths, Experiences, and Emotions." *Interpreting Women's Lives: Feminist Theory and Personal Narratives.* Ed. The Personal Narratives Group. Bloomington: Indiana University Press, 1998. 189–97.

"During the late 1940s . . . : Molasky, Michael. *The American Occupation of Japan and Okinawa: Literature and Memory.* London and New York: Routledge, 1999. 214. Also Dower, John. 134.

CHAPTER 27

put in charge of Negroes: B., Carter. Letters and Papers. 1900–1972. U.S. American Military History Institute. Carlisle, Pennsylvania.

orgy: Schanze, A.F. Papers. 1912–1962. "This was the Army." Senior Officers' Debriefing Program. ms. American Military History Institute. Carlisle, Pennsylvania. 1977.

his friend: S., Marvin. Telephone interview. 14 April 2007.

I find a form marked Secret: Execution of General Prisoner. Manila Provost Marshal Command 1 Dec 47. Supreme Commander for the Allied Powers. Legal Section. Manila Branch. (1945–11/1949); Records of Allied Operational and Occupation Headquarters, World War II, 1907–1966; Record Group 331; National Archives at College Park, College Park, MD.

Chaplain Oscar W. Schoech: Mahar, William. "Re: Search." Email to author. 24 July 2007.

Schoech is the subject: Buehner, Andrew J. "Chaplain Oscar w. Schoech Missionary to War Criminals." *Concordia Historical Institute Quarterly.* Vol 57, No.1 (1984).

Professor Lilly and Alice Kaplan mention: Lilly, J. Robert and J. Michael Thomson. "Executing U.S. Soldiers in England, WWII: The Power of Command Influence and Sexual Racism." Draft. 1995. 16 and Kaplan, Alice. 168–170.

CHAPTER 28

I read an order from Lieutenant General William Styer: Requisitions; File 371.2–413.44; Commanding General, U.S. Armed Forces, Western Pacific to the Commander in Chief Armed Forces Pacific, 10 April 1946; Provost Marshal General Correspondence 1946–1947. Record Group 554; National Archives at College Park, College Park, MD.

In the Eighth Army stockade's May report: Processing Work Sheet; 483rd Military Police Escort Guard Company; Records of Allied Operational and Occupation Headquarters, World War II, 1907–1966; Record Group 331; National Archives at College Park, College Park, MD.

A request for a report of execution: Report of Execution Form; "To HQ, General Prisoner Branch AFWESPAC Stockade" 7 August 1946. From Chief Provost Marshall, General Headquarters, US Army Forces, Pacific to General Prisoner Branch AFWESPAC Stockade; Records of General Headquarters; Provost Marshal Section, General Correspondence 1946–47; Record Group 389; National Archives at College Park, College Park, MD.

Tojo's executioner: Hartley, Robert. Personal interview. 8 Sep 2007.

Rexroad is: Martin, H.H. "Hanging is His Trade." *The Saturday Evening Post.* 5 June 1948.

Page 25 of the Provost Marshal's: Military Prisoners; Chapter VII; The Provost Marshal's History Campaigns of the Pacific 1941–1947; Provost Marshal's History Campaigns of the Pacific 1941–1947; Military Police Division Correspondence 1942–1947; Doctrine and Enforcement; Record Group 389; National Archives at College Park, College Park, MD.

An index shows a letter: Racial Incident; File 291.2; Cross Reference Index to the Series Central Decimal Correspondence Files, 1940–1945,' 1940–1945 and Central Decimal Correspondence Files, 1940–1945; War Department. The Adjutant General's Office. Record Group 407; National Archives at College Park, College Park, MD.

eighteen dishonorable discharges: List of Decedents PHILCOM Determined to be in "Dishonorable" Status, whose Cases are Being Processed and on when Disinterment Directives will be Issued at a Later Date; File 314.6; Correspondence Misc. File 1939–1954; Office of the Quartermaster General; Record Group 92; National Archives at College Park, College Park, MD.

the cemetery's keeper": Heilhecker, Larry. "Re: Clark Cemetery." Email to author. 24 May 2007.

The orders were given by telephone: Confinement of General Prisoners; Memorandum for Record 23 Aug 1947; General Headquarters; Far East Command; Office of the Provost Marshal; Provost Marshal General Correspondence, Supreme Commander for the Allied Powers,

1946–47. Record Group 554; National Archives at College Park, College Park, MD.

CHAPTER 29

Alice Kaplan . . . Lilly's research . . . moonshine . . . :
Lilly, J. Robert. 32. and Kaplan, Alice. 38, 67.

"the officer senior in rank often uses his weight . . .":
United States. House of Representatives Committee on Military Affairs. 17.

Walter Luszki's book: Luszki, Walter. 125–137.

"the uncertainties of reality . . .": Lesser, Wendy. *Pictures at an Execution.* Cambridge: Harvard University Press, 1993. 86.

a chance submission: Clark, Richard. "Shepton Mallet Prison in Somerset." *Capital Punishment U.K.* 16 Oct 2007. <http://www.richard.clark32.btinternet.co.uk/sheptonm.html>

list for those executed by the U.S. Air Force: "List of Those Executed by the United States Military." *Wikipedia.* 12 Oct 2007. <http://en.wikipedia.org/wiki/List_of_individuals_executed_by_the_United_States_military>

Burns and Dennis: M., William. "Re: Names. Email to author. 21 July 2007.

All the recorded courts-martial: U.S. Office of the JAG. *Holdings, Opinions, and Reviews: v.1–81 + 2 index volumes.* GPO, 1924–1949 and 1944–1949.

". . . not infrequently rejects or ignores it": United States. House of Representatives Committee on Military Affairs. 33.

immediately after the peace treaty was signed: Roehner, Bertrand M. *Relations Between Allied Forces and The Population of Japan 15 August 1945–31 December 1960.* Paris: University of Paris, 2007. 23.

dropped leaflets, derailed trains: Roehner, Bertrand M. 23–117.

They held many demonstrations: Roehner, Bertrand M. 77–117.

sixty-seven in the first three months: Roehner, Bertrand M. 80–81.

I wonder about the circumstances: Claims Against Estates; Report of Summary Court Officer File 250.414; 321: Infantry, September 1945–February 1946, 1945–1947 Supreme Commander for the Allied Powers. Adjutant General Section. Operations Division. Mail and Records Branch. Series: Classified Decimal File, 1945–1947. Record Group 331; National Archives at College Park, College Park, MD.

81 percent: Roehner, Bertrand M. 142.

cigarette scam: Roehner, Bertrand M. 57.

General Eichelberger twice: MacArthur, Douglas. Letter to All Unit Commanders. 22 June 1946. Entry A-1 135; File 250.1; Occupation Files 1945–1950; General Correspondence; Department of Defense. Far East Command. Eighth Army. Provost Marshal Section. Record Group 338; National Archives at College Park, College Park, MD. It begins "Since publishing my letter to you of 10 June regarding the behavior of our troops, I have received an increasing number of reports of crimes committed by Americans."

—Letter to Commanding General, Eighth Army. 8 Nov 1946. Entry A-1 135; File 250.1; Occupation Files 1945–1950; General Correspondence; Department of Defense. Far East Command. Eighth Army. Provost Marshal Section; Record Group 338; National Archives at College Park, College Park, MD. MacArthur complains in the letter that less than 50 percent of the reported rapes, assaults and robberies were investigated and only one-third of the burglaries. This is after receiving another letter from the Commanding General reporting alleged misconduct of occupational troops against Japanese Nationals for the month of September, 1946.

The National Archives houses the cover sheet: Roehner, Bertrand M. 72.

". . . high incidence of traffic accidents . . .": Roehner, Bertrand M. 88.

I too had noticed: Monthly Occupation Court Statistical Reports 1946–1949; Department of Defense; Far East Command; Eighth Army; Office of the Judge Advocate; Records of U.S. Army Operational, Tactical, and Support Organizations (World War II and Thereafter), 1917–1993; Record Group 338; National Archives at College Park, College Park, MD.

a New Zealand soldier: Bertrand M. 88.

even as late as April, 1952: Roehner, Bertrand M. 105.

The death toll: Roehner, Bertrand M. 140.

MacArthur censored newspapers: Roehner, Bertrand M. 15.

"Even the Allied military reports were subject to . . .": Roehner, Bertrand M. 17.

forbade mention of censorship: Roehner, Bertrand M. 28.

exiled or fired: Roehner, Bertrand M. 45–46.

Meanwhile the Stars and Stripes: "Hokkaido Trouble Greatly Exaggerated." *Pacific Stars and Stripes.* Tokyo, Japan. 12 May 1946.

how many U.S. soldiers died during the occupation: Roehner, Bertrand M. 136.

the British . . . showed a fatality rate: Roehner, Bertrand M. 141.

the same fatality rate . . . for American forces in Iraq: Roehner, Bertrand M. 138.

many more courts-martial: Roehner, Bertrand M. "Re: Occupation of Japan." Email to author. 7 Aug 2007.

"The so-called Military Government courts . . .": Roehner, Bertrand M. 80.

"The most tragic . . .": United States. House of Representatives Committee on Military Affairs. 43.

On May 25, 1946: Orr, E.B.. "What's Wrong with Military Justice?" *Christian Science Monitor.* 25 May 1946. 3.

CHAPTER 30

"omertà . . . the French use it . . .": Roehner, Bertrand M. "Re: Congratulations." Email to author. 9 Aug 2007.

shocking revelation: Turner, Major Lisa L. "The Articles of War and the UCMJ." *Aerospace Power Journal.* Fall 2000.

In May 2007: Aftergood, Steven. "Army Sees Gap in Jurisdiction Over Military Contractor." *Secrecy News: Federation of American Scientists Project on Government Secrecy.* 6 Apr 2007.

"Madame Butterfly's Children . . .": Kalischer, Peter. "Madame Butterfly's Children." *Collier's.* 20 Sep 1952. 17.

Only three are in marked graves: Sabin, Burritt. "They Came, They Saw, They Democratized." *Japan Times* 28 April 2002.

"I was arguing with myself . . .": Lifton, Robert Jay. *Home from the War–Vietnam Veterans: Neither Victims Nor Executioners.* New York: Basic Books, 1973. 121.

PHOTO CREDITS

p. 16 "Our biggest trouble was finding a place to go." "War Fire" from *Illustrated Nakano* 1985

p. 28 "Being lost in a big city like Tokyo . . ." *Soldiers Guide to Japan,* Eighth Army Printing Plant, c. 1946

p. 35 ". . . we would have been better off picking some younger, prettier girls." "Eiko Oshima" by Shomei Tomatsu, 1961. Reproduced with permission of the San Francisco Museum of Modern Art.

p. 46 "If you're a guard, getting prisoners quiet is the whole thing." "Solitary Confinement" by Wallace McGee

p. 60 "He said he was going to have to start executing the prisoners, the ones in the death cells." Eighth Army stockade, the Correction Library of the Japanese Correctional Association

p. 75 "Each prisoner had a transcript of his trial." Eighth Army stockade, the Correction Library of the Japanese Correctional Association

p. 77 "As the days rolled by, the idea that we are really going to execute the prisoners starts to sink in." Eighth Army stockade, the Correction Library of the Japanese Correctional Association

p. 84 "Guards . . . stared out the same bars." Ted Millette

p. 99 "Nakano's fame today rests on its anime and *manga* markets." Steve Bull

p. 111 ". . . designed in an X, the center of which is where the MPs slept." Ted Millette

p. 113 ". . . the little red-caped and bibbed statues." Steve Bull

p. 119 "How lonely she is!" Steve Bull

p. 129 "A good-looking man walking a small dog." Steve Bull

p. 144 "More smoke." Eighth Army stockade, the Correction Library of the Japanese Correctional Association

p. 144 "MPs don't like to keep records." National Archives

p. 145 "I find two of the three "Greens." National Personnel Records Center

p. 149 "Smoke." Eighth Army stockade, the Correction Library of the Japanese Correctional Association

p. 165 "I only know what he told me." From the collection of Frank Svoboda

p. 179 "More smoke." Eighth Army stockade, the Correction Library of the Japanese Correctional Association

p. 188 "Time to Add a Few Pages?" *The Christian Science Monitor,* May 25, 1946. From the article "What's Wrong with Military Justice?" by E. B. Orr, p. 3. Copyright © 1946 *The Christian Science Monitor* (www.csmonitor.com). All rights reserved.

ACKNOWLEDGMENTS

First of all, I would like to thank Robert Polito for having chosen my book (and for his definition of *mystery*). Thanks so much to so many so often that they are jumbled all together: Max Friedman, Mary Sherman Willis, Lieutenant Colonel Bob Bateman, Leslie Daniels, Dave Gibson, Katherine Gibson, Julie Graham, John E. Taylor at the National Archives, Jonathan Keats, Sheri Geyelin, Laurie Stone, Dean Dominic J. Balestra, Joyce George, Sammy Popat, Frederic Smoler, Major Peter Knight at West Point, James W. Zobel at the MacArthur Memorial, Ron Sherman, Hikaru Kasahara, Hidemitsu Nagani at the Chuoh Library of Nakano City, Fordham's interlibrary-loan librarian, Charlotte Labbe, Fordham's reference librarian, Nancy Stout, Nakano Ward History Resources Museum, Nakano Historical Museum, Bill Barrette, Peace Materials Exhibition Room, the Correctional Library of the Japanese Correctional Association, Alice Kaplan, Robert Lilly, David A. Keough and Robert Mages at the U.S. Army Military History Institute, Dr. Craig at the U.S. Army MP Corps Museum, Luther Hanson from the Department of Justice, Sondra Olson, Gay Walley, Delores Svoboda, Chris Svoboda, Craig and Sarah Howes, Colonel Robin N. Swope, Dan Lavering, Matt Weiland, Robert Dreesen, Steve Bull, and of course, my dear father, Frank Svoboda.

THE GRAYWOLF PRESS NONFICTION PRIZE

Black Glasses Like Clark Kent: A GI's Secret from Postwar Japan by Terese Svoboda is the 2007 winner of the Graywolf Press Nonfiction Prize. Graywolf awards this prize annually to a previously unpublished, full-length work of outstanding literary nonfiction by a writer who is not yet established in the genre. The 2006 winner was *Neck Deep and Other Predicaments* by Ander Monson and the 2005 winner was *Frantic Transmissions to and from Los Angeles: An Accidental Memoir* by Kate Braverman.

The Graywolf Press Nonfiction Prize seeks to acknowledge—and honor—the great traditions of literary nonfiction, extending from Robert Burton and Thomas Browne in the seventeenth century through Daniel Defoe and Lytton Strachey and on to James Baldwin, Joan Didion, and Jamaica Kincaid in our own time. Whether grounded in observation, autobiography, or research, much of the most beautiful, daring, and original writing over the past few decades can be categorized as nonfiction. Graywolf is excited to increase its commitment to the evolving and dynamic genre.

The prize is judged by Robert Polito, author of *Savage Art: A Biography of Jim Thompson, Doubles,* and *A Reader's Guide to James Merrill's "The Changing Light at Sandover,"* and director of the graduate writing program at the New School, in New York City.

The Graywolf Press Nonfiction Prize is funded in part by endowed gifts from the Arsham Ohanessian Charitable Remainder Unitrust and the Ruth Easton Fund of the Edelstein Family Foundation.

Arsham Ohanessian, an Armenian born in Iraq who came to the United States in 1952, was an avid reader and a tireless advocate for human rights and peace. He strongly believed in the power of literature and education to make a positive impact on humanity.

Ruth Easton, born in North Branch, Minnesota, was a Broadway actress in the 1920s and 1930s. The Ruth Easton Fund of the Edelstein Family Foundation is pleased to support the work of emerging artists and writers in her honor.

Graywolf Press is grateful to Arsham Ohanessian and Ruth Easton for their generous support.

TERESE SVOBODA has published nine books of prose and poetry, most recently *Tin God.* Svoboda's writing has been featured in the *New Yorker,* the *New York Times,* the *Atlantic, Slate, Bomb, Columbia, Yale Review,* and the *Paris Review.* She lives in New York. Visit her web site: www.teresesvoboda.com.

The text of *Black Glasses Like Clark Kent* has been typeset in Concorde, a font designed by Günter Gerhard Lange in 1967. Book design by Wendy Holdman. Composition at Prism Publishing Center. Manufactured by Versa Press on acid-free paper.